KEYS TO UNDERSTANDING THE FINANCIAL NEWS

Second Edition

Nicholas G. Apostolou, DBA, CPA
Professor of Accounting
Louisiana State University
Baton Rouge, Louisiana

D. Larry Crumbley, PhD, CPA
Deborah D. Shelton Taxation Professor
Texas A & M University
College Station, Texas

BARRON'S

ACKNOWLEDGMENTS

Authors and publisher express their appreciation to the following individuals and companies for permission to reprint material: Dow Jones & Company, for excerpts from *The Wall Street Journal*; Ibbotson Associates; and the Chicago Board Options Exchange.

All inquiries should be addressed to:
Barron's Educational Series, Inc.
250 Wireless Boulevard
Hauppauge, New York 11788

Library of Congress Catalog Card No. 93-23233

International Standard Book No. 0-8120-1694-7

Library of Congress Cataloging-in-Publication Data
Apostolou, Nicholas G.
    Keys to understanding the financial news / Nicholas G. Apostolou, D. Larry Crumbley.—2nd ed.
        p.   cm.—(Barron's business keys)
    Includes bibliographical references and index.
    ISBN 0-8120-1694-7
    1. Finance. 2. Newspapers—Sections, columns, etc.—Finance.
I. Crumbley, D. Larry. II. Title. III. Series.
HG173.A75 1994
070.4'49332—dc20   93-23233
                                                                      CIP

PRINTED IN THE UNITED STATES OF AMERICA
567   9692   9876543

CONTENTS

1

OVERVIEW OF THE NEWS

People are bombarded with financial and economic information on a daily basis. Reports on such items as the GDP, unemployment rate, consumer price index, and the money supply are publicized not only in the financial news but also in our local newspapers. Anyone reading the financial pages is faced with a bewildering array of stock tables, price quotes, and predictions of future trends, often contradictory in nature. The concerned nonexpert may find it a daunting task to synthesize and integrate this information so as to make specific economic decisions.

This book is for those individuals who wish to understand the implications of the financial news. This understanding does not require you to be an expert. Rather, the goal is to permit you to make an informed appraisal of the information reported in local newspapers, national financial newspapers such as *The Wall Street Journal* and *Investor's Business Daily*, television, weekly financial publications such as *Barron's,* and the business periodicals such as *Business Week*, *Forbes*, and *Fortune*.

This book is by no stretch of the imagination a theoretical treatment of finance, economics, or investments. For example, textbooks that deal with economics can be dull and forbidding, and they generally fail to provide elementary information on when economic information is reported and how you should interpret that information in making economic decisions.

Similarly, most finance and investment books are either too theoretical or too personal, espousing the author's system of amassing riches. This book does not provide you with a foolproof system of becoming wealthy. Rather, it presents fundamental material from the areas of economics, finance, and investments to enable you to interpret the financial news with a little common sense and sophistication. In this way, you can form your own opinions about current economic and business events rather than looking for so-called experts to interpret them.

We are not suggesting that you dispense with expert advice. The point is to form your own opinion based upon the facts, so that you are better able to judge the validity of the advice of others. Otherwise, you don't have an independent check on other opinions.

The book is organized around "keys" to understanding the financial news. The purpose of each of these discussions is to provide you with sufficient information to interpret the financial news and make economic decisions. It is a practical how-to book, rather than a theoretical or conceptual discussion. Specific examples are presented from the daily press to illuminate discussion of the keys. Further, at the end of the book, a glossary is presented along with a series of the most commonly asked questions and answers to these questions.

2

GROSS DOMESTIC PRODUCT

Gross Domestic Product (GDP) represents the total market value of the final output of a nation's goods and services produced within the boundaries of the United States, whether by American or foreign-supplied resources. It was formerly called the Gross National Product (GNP). Most nations today use GDP as the principal measure of their output. In 1992, the United States changed from GNP accounting to GDP. The GDP is the broadest single measure of U.S. economic activity and is usually considered to be the best available indicator of the economy's health. As a result, it receives strong media interest. These GDP reports are percentage changes reported as an annual rate. For example, on April 30, 1993, the change in GDP was estimated as an annual growth rate of 1.8% in the first quarter.

The U.S. Department of Commerce issues quarterly estimates of GDP during the third week of January, April, July, and October. In addition, there are usually "flash" or preliminary reports that give a rough estimate of GDP sometime prior to the end of each quarter. About one year later, after more data become available, the Department of Commerce issues an official figure, which is often substantially different from the estimated figure.

In 1993, the GDP of the U.S. economy will exceed $6 trillion. This figure represents a substantial increase over the 1985 GDP of $4.04 trillion. However, about a third of this growth results from inflation rather than representing a real increase in the output of goods and services.

The measurement of GDP involves productive transactions only—the final purchase of newly produced goods or services. Excluded are nonproductive transactions, which can be broken down into two categories: financial transactions,

3

such as buying and selling of securities, government transfer payments (Social Security, etc.) and private transfer payments (gifts), and the transfer of used goods.

GDP can be broken down into four components:

1. Personal consumption expenditures
2. Government expenditures
3. Gross private domestic investment
4. Net exports

Personal consumption expenditures include expenditures by households on consumer goods and services. *Government expenditures* include federal, state, and local governmental spending on the finished products of businesses plus all direct purchases of resources by government. *Gross private domestic* investment refers to investment spending by business firms in future productive capacity, including changes in inventory.

GDP is also increased by *net exports:* the production of goods and services that are exported decreased by the total value of imported goods, which do not reflect productive activity in the U.S. economy (see Key 12, BALANCE OF TRADE). If the value of the exports is less than the value of the imports, the figure is negative, reducing the GDP.

These four components add up to GDP. The equation that represents this relationship is:

$$GDP = C + I + G + NE$$

where C = consumption expenditures,
     I = investment expenditures,
     G = government expenditures,
  NE = total exports minus total imports.

Adjusting Gross Domestic Product. Because of the effects of inflation, comparisons of GDP for different years using the reported numbers can be misleading. GDP can be adjusted by expressing it in terms of real purchasing power using a particular year as a standard of comparison. When GDP is corrected for changes in prices, it is called "real" GDP. If GDP is expressed in current dollars without adjusting for price changes, it is referred to as "nominal" GDP.

A more meaningful measure of economic well-being for many purposes is to compute GDP on a per-capita basis. For example, if real GDP had increased by 15% over a ten-year period during which the population had increased by 25%, the nation's citizens would be less well off than previously. To adjust for changes in population, real GDP can be divided by population to obtain per capita real GDP.

Deficiencies of Gross Domestic Product. Although GDP is designed to measure the total value of all goods and services produced in the economy, certain activities are not included by government statisticians. Productive do-it-yourself activities are not included in GDP because these transactions are not reflected in the marketplace. Of even greater significance is the omission of services performed by individuals in the home. These services would be included if performed by a housekeeper. Finally, illegal activities such as narcotics dealing, gambling, and prostitution are not included in the calculation of GDP. Unreported activities may account for 20% of measured GDP, and they are growing faster than the reported activities. The greater the significance of the underground economy relative to total economic activity, the more the reported amount of GDP may be underestimating the true value of total output.

3

LEADING ECONOMIC INDICATORS

Around the first of each month, the U.S. Department of Commerce publishes three indicators of business activity. The index that receives the most widespread media attention is the Index of Leading Economic Indicators. The other two indexes are the Index of Coincident Economic Indicators and the Index of Lagging Economic Indicators. These indicators are published in *Survey of Current Business*, an indispensable publication for anyone interested in evaluating economic activity. The indicators are listed in Exhibit 1.

The leading indicators are important because investors are more interested in the future path of the economy than they are in what is happening currently (coincident indicators) or what has happened (lagging indicators). The leading indicators are not completely reliable. In fact, more than one third of the time they give false signals. The leading indicators generally peak about five months before a recession, but this varies. The index peaked about eight months before the recessions of 1969–70 and 1974 but only three months before the recession of 1981–82. Overall, the index has been more successful at anticipating recoveries than in predicting recessions. Many economists believe that the index of leading indicators needs a major overhaul. They find it increasingly less relevant to the economy's actual performance or prospects. Geoffrey Moore, head of the Center for International Business Cycle Research at Columbia University, has cited several deficiencies in the index that impair its usefulness. For example, the U.S. Department of Commerce includes in its monthly series on "contracts and orders for plant and equipment" only orders received at firms

6

EXHIBIT 1

Economic Indicators

Leading Economic Indicators

1. Average weekly hours paid to production workers in manufacturing.
2. Average weekly claims for unemployment insurance.
3. New orders for consumer goods and materials.
4. Index of 500 common stock prices.
5. Contracts and orders for new plant and equipment.
6. Index of building permits for new private housing units.
7. Vendor performance — slower deliveries index.
8. Change in index of sensitive materials.
9. Money supply (M2).
10. Change in manufacturers' unfilled orders (in 1982 dollars).
11. Index of consumer expectations.

Coincident Economic Indicators

1. Employees on nonagricultural payrolls.
2. Index of industrial production.
3. Personal income minus transfer payments.
4. Manufacturing, wholesale, and retail sales.

Lagging Economic Indicators

1. Index of labor cost per unit of output in manufacturing.
2. Ratio of manufacturing and trade inventory to sales.
3. Average duration of unemployment.
4. Ratio of consumer installment debt to personal income.
5. Commercial and industrial loans outstanding.
6. Average prime interest rate charged by banks.
7. Change in consumer price index for services.

operating in the United States. This computation ignores U.S. imports of capital goods. Moore maintains that a broader index that would include imports as well as orders placed domestically could be easily constructed.

In addition, Moore laments the fact that the service sector, which is becoming increasingly important in the economy, is underrepresented. An examination of the 11 leading indicators in Exhibit 1 shows that they primarily relate to the production and manufacture of goods.

How to Use the Index. The Index of Leading Economic Indicators can be thought of as a useful but not totally reliable predicting tool. The rule of thumb is that three successive monthly declines, or increases, in the index indicate that the economy will soon turn in the same direction. Remember that monthly moves in the index are not as important as the cumulative long-run trend.

4

INFLATION

Between 1968 and 1993, the general level of prices as measured by the Consumer Price Index more than quadrupled. Inflation has become an economic fact of American life, and no reputable forecaster assumes that this condition will change in the future. Inflation causes great concern because it results in the redistribution of wealth when it is not anticipated. For example, inflation tends to benefit borrowers at the expense of lenders whenever inflation rates are underestimated over the life of a loan. If $10,000 is borrowed for one year and the inflation rate for that year is 5%, the dollars of principal repaid at the end of the year have depreciated by 5%. The borrower benefits by repaying less real dollars, while the lender receives dollars whose purchasing power has declined. Hence, inflation causes the lender to lose.

Inflation can also have a corrosive effect on savings. As prices rise, the value of savings will decline if the rate of inflation exceeds the rate of interest. People on fixed incomes are hurt by inflation. The workers who retired in 1982 on a fixed pension found that by 1993 the purchasing power of their monthly check had declined by about 50%.

Measuring Inflation. If inflation is defined as a rise in the general level of prices, how is it measured? This problem is easily solved when referring to the price change of one good, but it becomes trickier when dealing with a large number of goods, some with prices that have risen faster than others. Realistically, price changes for all the goods produced by the economy cannot be computed. Instead, statisticians for the federal government have selected a representative market basket of goods and then computed the price changes of the market basket every month.

One way to gain an appreciation for the effect of inflation is to employ the "rule of 72." This method provides an approximate measure of the number of years required for the price level to double. The number 72 is divided by the annual rate of inflation:

$$\text{Number of years required for prices to double} = \frac{72}{\text{annual rate of inflation}}$$

For example, the price level will double in approximately 14 years if the inflation rate is 5% per year. Similarly, inflation of 10% per year means the price level will double in about seven years. Savers can use this formula to estimate how long it will take their savings to double.

Prominent Price Indexes. Three price indexes calculated by government statisticians receive a great deal of attention in the financial press: the Consumer Price Index (CPI), the Producer Price Index (PPI), and the Gross Domestic Product (GDP) Deflator. Each of these indexes measures the average price change for the goods and services that comprise the index. The changes in these indexes are highly correlated over time, and each reveals the persistence of inflation in recent economic history.

The Consumer Price Index. The CPI is the most widely cited index in the media. It attempts to measure changes in the prices of goods and services purchased by urban consumers. The Bureau of Labor Statistics computes the index monthly based upon data collected in 85 cities on the price changes of approximately 400 goods and services in seven broad categories: food, clothing, housing, transportation, medical care, entertainment, and other. The CPI is considered to be the most reliable measure of changes in the cost of living for most American families. For the CPI, prices for 1982–1984 represent the base year, which is set at 100. For example, the CPI measured in 1993 was 40% more than the level of 1982.

Producer Price Index. The PPI, formerly called the Wholesale Price Index, measures changes in the average prices of goods received by producers of commodities, in all stages of processing, in primary or wholesale markets. It measures the change in prices paid by businesses rather than by consumers. The market basket for calculating the PPI consists of about 3200 items purchased by producers and manufacturers including crude, intermediate, and finished goods (see Exhibit 2).

Because primary products included in the PPI are processed into finished goods distributed to retail markets, many analysts believe that changes in the PPI precede changes in the CPI. For this reason, the PPI is closely followed as a leading indicator of consumer prices. However, this relationship does not always hold true. Because the PPI does not include services, the price changes of CPI and PPI may not correlate when the price of services changes at a rate that is different from the rate for other price changes.

Gross Domestic Product Deflator. The GDP deflator is the most broadly based of the price level indicators. It includes price changes on not only goods and services that households purchase (about two thirds of GDP), but also expenditures by government, investment by business, and purchases by the foreign sector. Thus the GDP deflator measures the prices of all final goods and services.

The GDP deflator is calculated as a by-product of the calculation of current and real GDP. It is obtained by dividing current-year quantities at current-year prices by current-year quantities at base-year prices. (The base year is currently 1987.) Unlike the CPI and the PPI, which are reported monthly, both the GDP and the GDP deflator are calculated and reported quarterly.

EXHIBIT 2

Example Reporting of the
Producer Price Index
PRODUCER PRICES

Here are the Labor Department's producer price indexes (1982 = 100) for March, before seasonal adjustment, and the percentage changes from March, 1992.

Finished goods	124.6	2.0%
Minus food & energy	136.2	1.9%
Intermediate goods	115.9	2.0%
Crude goods	102.6	4.8%

Source: *The Wall Street Journal*

Over the years common stocks have been a better inflation hedge than bonds or Treasury Securities. As a general proposition, lower inflation leads to higher returns for stocks and bonds, while higher inflation reduces returns on stocks and bonds. Bonds with longer-term maturities are particularly risky when inflation unexpectedly heats up. Physical goods or assets such as real estate, precious metals, art objects, and collectibles have been excellent inflation hedges. However, the declines in the prices of gold and silver in the late 1980s show there are no guarantees that even real assets will continue to outstrip the rate of inflation.

Future Trends in Inflation. What should the investor look for in the news to appraise the future prospects of inflation? Two good indicators to watch are the unemployment rate (see Key 10) and the capacity-utilization, or factory-operating, rate.

Capacity utilization measures what manufacturers currently produce as compared to the most they could produce. It provides you with an excellent indication of whether the economy is operating near full capacity. Rising capacity use rates indicate increasing pressure on the economy's resource base. Higher utilization brings less efficient, higher cost capacity into production and is often accompanied by tighter labor markets that put further upward pressure on wages.

The Federal Reserve closely watches this indicator, and investors should also. When capacity utilization exceeds 85%, inflation becomes a threat to the economy. The Fed releases this indicator in the third week of every month.

The PPI is the first inflation report to be published each month. Although the PPI and CPI can provide widely different measures of inflation in an individual month, over time they are highly correlated. Don't read too much into one period's results. Note the trend and decide whether or not a new direction is indicated.

5

FEDERAL RESERVE SYSTEM

The Federal Reserve System is a complex organization that includes the Board of Governors of the Federal Reserve System, the Federal Open Market Committee, and the 12 regional Federal Reserve Banks. The Federal Reserve (Fed) is the central bank, and it has many functions, as outlined below. Although the Fed does not control interest rates, it can significantly influence interest rates through control of the money supply. Its importance in our financial system is pervasive, and knowledge of its purposes and functions is critical to investors.

Structure of the Fed. At the top of the Federal Reserve's organization structure is the Board of Governors. The primary function of the Board is the formulation of monetary policy; in addition, the Board has broad responsibilities for the activities of national and state-chartered member banks. The seven members of the Board are appointed by the President and confirmed by the Senate. All appointments are for 14-year terms, theoretically insulating the Board from short-term political influence. The President also designates the chairman and the vice chairman, who serve for four-year terms with redesignation possible as long as their terms as Board members have not expired. The chairman of the Board occupies a powerful position, often cited as being second only to that of the President.

Implementation of Monetary Policy. The most important responsibility of the Fed is the control of the money supply. The principal tools the Fed can use to regulate the money supply are:

1. *Open Market Operations:* The most important policy instrument of the Fed and involves buying and selling

U.S. Government securities in the open market. Decisions are made by the Federal Open Market Committee, consisting of the seven members of the Board of Governors, the president of the Federal Reserve Bank of New York, and four other presidents of Reserve Banks. The financial community closely monitors these activities. Banks are required to maintain cash reserves against the money they loan. The larger a bank's reserves, the more money it is able to loan, and the more money a bank is able to lend, the larger the money supply tends to be. When the Fed purchases securities (e.g., Treasury bills), and the seller is an individual or nonbank corporation, the seller generally deposits the check in a commercial bank, which presents it to the Fed for credit. This increases the reserves of the bank, permitting it to increase the money available to lend.

Conversely, when the Fed sells securities, the opposite occurs. A nonbank buyer pays the Fed with checks drawn on a bank. The Fed deducts this check from the bank's reserve balance, and the bank has less money to lend, restricting growth in the money supply. Thus, purchase of securities raise bank reserves while Fed sales of securities lower reserves. The effect is immediate and the adjustment of reserves is precise. The Fed employs this method daily as needed.

2. *Discount Window:* Discounting occurs when the Fed lends reserves to member banks. The rate of interest the Fed charges is called the discount rate. The rate is altered periodically as market conditions change or to complement open market operations. It is primarily of interest as an indication of the Federal Reserve's view of the economy and money and credit demand.

3. *Reserve Requirements:* Banks are required to maintain reserves against the money they loan. When reserve requirements are increased, the amount of deposits supported by the supply of reserves is reduced and banks have to reduce their loans. Although this tool is powerful, it is less flexible than the other two policy instruments and, therefore, is seldom used.

Effect of Fed Action. On May 24, 1993, Federal Reserve officials, concerned about signs that inflationary pressures were building, voted to lean toward higher short-term interest rates. With this action, the Fed indicated its resolve to raise interest rates if inflation threatened to intensify. Rising interest rates heighten investor concern because the higher the interest debt that securities pay, the more attractive they become to investors as compared to stocks, thereby encouraging the flow of funds from stocks to bonds.

The investment adviser Edson Gould formalized this concern over 40 years ago when he developed a trading rule called "three steps and a stumble." As he put it, three consecutive tightening moves by the Fed signals a coming downturn in stock prices. Though popular with investors and widely publicized in the media, Gould's rule does not hold up to analysis. In the last 50 years, the discount rate has been raised three times in a row on eight occasions. Although each time the market fell, on six of those occasions stock prices were up six months later.

More critical to the course of the market is investors' confidence that the Fed will be able to contain inflation without bringing on a damaging recession. The Fed continually faces a delicate balancing act, for if it raises rates too much, corporate profits and economic activity will suffer, and if it fails to act strongly enough, rising inflation will result.

6

MONEY SUPPLY

The definition of the money supply causes economists continuing problems. The Federal Reserve has periodically redefined its definitions of money because of the emergence of new types of financial instruments such as Negotiable Orders of Withdrawal (NOW) accounts, Repurchase Agreements (RPs or REPOs), and Money Market Deposit Accounts (MMDAs). Currently, the Fed has subdivided the money supply into four categories: Ml, M2, M3, L.

Ml is currency in circulation plus all checking accounts including those that pay interest, such as NOW accounts. Ml is the narrowest definition of the money supply and it represents money primarily held to carry out transactions. Over 70% represents demand deposits, while less than 30% consists of currency and coin.

M2 expands M1 to include items that are not quite as liquid, including:

1. RPs or REPOs, which are agreements made by banks to sell government securities to customers and, simultaneously, to repurchase the same securities at a price that includes accumulated interest. RPs offer a way to earn interest on idle cash.
2. Certain short-term deposits at Caribbean branches of member banks held by U.S. nonbank residents.
3. Money market mutual fund (MMMF) balances.
4. Money market deposit accounts (MMDAs).
5. Savings and small-denomination time deposits (e.g., CDs) of less than $100,000.

M3 is the broadest measure of the money supply, adding to M2 other liquid assets that are owned predominantly by wealthy individuals and institutions. Examples include:

1. Time deposits and certain other instruments through which funds are loaned in large denominations ($100,000 or more) to depository institutions.
2. Eurodollars held by U.S. residents.
3. Shares in money market funds that are generally restricted to institutions.

Debt by depository institutions in these forms represents funds that can be readily managed and varied in line with changes in fund needs.

The Fed also publishes a broader measure of liquidity called L. This measure includes a variety of short-term market instruments. Examples are:

1. Banker's acceptances.
2. Commercial paper.
3. Marketable Treasury and agency obligations with original maturities of less than 12 months.

This measure has not served as a target for monetary policy because data on it are not promptly available.

Significance of the Money Supply. The supply of money is of crucial importance to economic activity. The money supply is one of the most useful leading indicators (see Key 3). In addition, it is also used by many analysts for insight into the future course of stock prices. Changes in the total money supply and the rate at which it increases or decreases affect important economic variables such as the inflation rate, interest rate, employment, and gross domestic product. The control of the money supply is the primary responsibility of the Fed (see Key 5). An increase in the money supply relative to demand for it causes interest rates to fall, stimulating investment spending, output, and employment.

Particularly when resources are fully employed, an increasing money supply has inflationary consequences. When more money exists than is needed to carry out transactions, inflation will result. However, inflation doesn't immediately follow an acceleration in money growth. The process has historically taken from one and one-half to two years, although in recent years changes in the money supply have been a less reliable indicator of future inflation. Monetary indicators may have become less reliable in predicting future inflation because of the recent introduction of new financial instruments such as NOW accounts, RPs, and MMDAs. In the summer of 1993, the Fed announced that it would put less emphasis on changes in the money supply as the basis for making its decisions on use of monetary tools.

Reporting the M's. The money supply numbers are reported every Thursday afternoon. "Fed watchers" analyze these numbers for clues to the direction of monetary policy. Although Ml receives the greatest attention in the media, M2 is more closely watched by most economists. M2 is also the money supply number included in the leading economic indicators.

7

INTEREST RATES

The interest rate is the price a borrower pays for the use of a lender's money. Interest is usually expressed as an annual rate or percentage rather than as an absolute amount. Thus, if an individual borrows $100 for one year, a payment of $10 on the amount borrowed translates to a 10% annual simple interest. Interest rates are usually set by market forces and vary greatly in differing circumstances. A loan to buy a house may cost the borrower 6% to 9% annual interest. Department store and bank charge cards typically charge 18% to 23% annual interest. However, the federal government usually pays 4% to 8% interest on its debt. Variations in the interest paid result from many factors, including length of loans, risk to the lender, and administrative costs. (See Exhibit 3.)

Real Versus Nominal Interest Rates. The nominal interest rate is the rate of interest expressed in current dollars. Inflation causes the nominal interest rate to be higher, as the rate rises to reflect the anticipated rate of inflation. The real interest rate is obtained by subtracting the anticipated rate of inflation from the nominal rate of interest. If the nominal rate of interest is 5% and the rate of inflation is 5%, the real rate of interest is zero.

Panoply of Interest Rates. Although all interest rates tend to move in the same direction at the same time, an examination of the financial pages reveals there are dozens of different interest rates. Some of the most widely quoted interest rates are:

1. *Federal Funds Rate:* the rate banks have to pay to borrow reserves from other banks. A rise in the federal funds rate indicates that more banks are running short of reserves, while a fall indicates the opposite. This rate also provides an indication of Federal Reserve monetary

EXHIBIT 3

Money Rates and Yield Curve

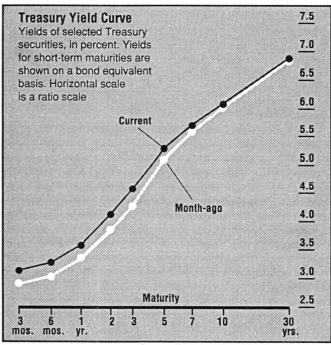

Treasury Yield Curve
Yields of selected Treasury securities, in percent. Yields for short-term maturities are shown on a bond equivalent basis. Horizontal scale is a ratio scale

Current

Month-ago

Maturity

3 mos. 6 mos. 1 yr. 2 3 5 7 10 30 yrs.

7.5 7.0 6.5 6.0 5.5 5.0 4.5 4.0 3.5 3.0 2.5

Source: Technical Data, The New York Times

Key Rates (in percent)	Yesterday	Previous Day	Year Ago
Prime Rate	6.00	6.00	6.50
Discount Rate	3.00	3.00	3.50
Federal Funds*	3.38	3.02	3.89
3-Mo. Treas. Bills	3.08	3.05	3.72
6-Mo. Treas. Bills	3.22	3.20	3.85
7-Yr. Treas. Notes	5.67	5.78	6.97
30-Yr. Treas. Bonds	6.88	6.98	7.86
Telephone Bonds	7.82	7.92	8.70
Municipal Bonds**	5.88	5.89	6.65

*Estimated daily average, source Telerate
**Municipal Bond Index, The Bond Buyer
Salomon Brothers and Telerate for Treasury's bell-wether bonds, notes and bills

policy. A rising trend in the rate signals a more restrictive policy, while a fall indicates a more expansionary policy. However, sharp fluctuations can occur from one day to the next without signalling a change in policy.

2. *Prime rate:* the rate charged by commercial banks to their most creditworthy business customers. Businesses that are less creditworthy are charged a higher interest rate. The prime rate is a bellwether rate in the sense that when it is raised, many other interest rates will rise. Alternatively, a reduction in the prime rate signals a decline in interest rates.

3. *Commercial paper rate:* the rate on short-term, unsecured (i.e., no collateral) debt issued by large corporations and other borrowers to investors with surplus cash. The interest rate is usually less than that charged by banks.

4. *Mortgage rate:* the rate charged by thrift institutions to home buyers. Up to 90% of the cost of a home is usually borrowed and repaid in monthly installments over 15 to 30 years. A climb in mortgage rates raises monthly payments and has a depressing effect on new home construction.

5. *Treasury bill rate:* the rate on short-term securities that mature in three months, six months, or one year and are issued in minimum denominations of $10,000 with $5,000 increments. Treasury bills are sold at a discount from face value and are redeemed at full face value upon maturity. Since they are guaranteed by the full faith and credit of the U.S. government, they are the safest of securities.

6. *Bond rate:* these rates depend upon the length of the bond term and the creditworthiness of the issuer. Generally speaking, bonds that mature in 30 years pay a higher rate than bonds maturing in 10 years. The reason is that price fluctuates with changes in the level of interest rates, increasing the risk of capital loss over the longer term. Treasury bonds pay less interest than corporate bonds because, like Treasury bills and notes, they are guaranteed by the full faith and credit of the U.S. government. Treasury bonds range in maturity

from 10 to 30 years and are issued in $1,000 minimum denominations, with $5,000, $10,000, $50,000, $100,000, and $1 million denominations also available.

Yield Curve. The yield curve results from a graph that plots the interest rates of short-term and long-term Treasury securities. Thus it shows in graphic form the relationship between maturity and a security's yield at a point in time.

As a rule, the yield curve slopes upward because interest rates usually rise with the length of the investment. The logic is simple: if investors commit their money for more time, they take more risk and demand a greater return. In unusual situations, when short-term Treasury securities yield higher rates than long-term bonds, there is an inverted yield curve, one that slopes downward.

The yield curve generally inverts when the Fed raises interest rates to slow down the economy and control inflation. The market sees the Fed fighting inflation, and this reduces inflationary expectations, dampening the rate on long-term bonds. Typically, an inverted yield curve indicates that the market expects interest rates to decline in the future, accompanied by an economic contraction. What are the signs that interest rates are going to decline? Watch the trend in the federal funds rate. By setting the rate, the Fed effectively determines all short-term interest rates.

The link between the money markets and long-term interest rates is more tenuous. Long-term interest rates are primarily affected by inflationary expectations. Therefore, changes in short-term rates may not always correspond to changes in long-term rates. However, the Fed's clout should not be underestimated. If the Fed is aggressively easing or tightening credit, long-term rates will move in the same direction as short-term rates do.

8

FISCAL POLICY

Fiscal policy refers to the federal government's policy in regard to taxation and spending. Fiscal policy is often differentiated from monetary policy, which refers to the actions of the Federal Reserve.

Discretionary fiscal policy is defined as a deliberate change in the rate of taxation and/or government spending by the federal government for the purpose of lowering unemployment or inflation. The federal government has the option of increasing or reducing governmental expenditures, raising or lowering taxes, or using a combination of the two to stabilize the economy. An expansionary fiscal policy should be employed when a recession occurs. Such a policy involves increasing government spending, or lowering taxes, or a combination of the two.

If inflation is of concern, a contractionary fiscal policy should be implemented. Such a policy consists of decreasing government spending, or raising taxes, or a combination of the two. Ideally, the federal government should attempt to achieve a budget surplus when the unemployment rate is low and the economy is faced with the problem of runaway inflation.

Supply-side Economics. At least in the first years of the Reagan administration, supply-side economics had great influence over policymakers. The underlying assumption of supply-side economics is that individuals, in their capacities as workers, savers, and investors, will respond to changes in marginal tax rates. The higher the marginal tax rate, the greater the incentive to avoid paying taxes, either through legal tax avoidance, illegal tax evasion, or less work, saving, and investment. Alternatively, a reduction in marginal tax rates should actually increase tax revenues. This was the reasoning behind the tax cut of 1981.

Since supply-siders did not believe that, aside from taxes, fiscal policy was very important, they did not cut planned government spending as much as tax revenues. Thus government expenditures continued to rise as a percentage of GDP even though tax revenues stabilized. This increased the Federal deficit dramatically.

It was clearly a mistake to cut taxes without cutting total government expenditures at the same time. Nevertheless, except for the large deficits, supply-side policies were not unsuccessful. In response to tax incentives, investment spending rose rapidly after 1982, and the economy continued to generate a large number of new jobs while prices rose slowly.

Monetary Policy Versus Fiscal Policy. Any discussion of fiscal policy has to grapple with the fact that it doesn't seem to work as advertised. Empirical testing has not found any correlation between the surplus or deficit and current or future economic activity. Increases in deficits have been followed by several recessions, and huge deficits have been accompanied by substantial unemployment, violating the theory of fiscal policy. A school of thought called monetarism asserts that changes in the supply of money are the determinants of economic activity. Monetarists focus upon the Fed as the most important player in determining the future course of the economy. They argue that fiscal policy is impotent in affecting future levels of economic activity. Although the debate about the importance of monetary policy versus fiscal policy continues, monetarists have clearly impressed upon the financial community the importance of the Fed and its control over the money supply.

When monetary policy is eased, interest rates fall, raising bond prices, and stocks become more attractive because investors expect faster economic growth and higher corporate profits. Conversely, rising interest rates reduce bond prices and eventually slow economic growth and reduce corporate profits. Stock investors should remember that over the past 23 years (1959–1992), the S&P has gained 22% a year during periods when monetary policy was easing, but only 0.3% a year in periods of monetary tightening.

9

MEASURES OF PRODUCTIVITY

Productivity measures are measures of efficiency in the use of resources. Productivity is defined as the average physical output produced per unit of input in any given time period. The greater the output produced from a given amount of inputs, the more productive is the economy. The key measure of productivity for the economy is labor productivity, which is defined as the ratio of real output to labor input measured in hours paid. In equation form:

$$\text{Labor Productivity} = \frac{\text{Output}}{\text{Hours paid}} = \frac{\text{Average output}}{\text{Per hour}}$$

The importance of this ratio cannot be overstated. This measure is the most important indicator of the nation's efficiency. Real income and the standard of living of the population cannot increase without an increase in the productivity of the labor force.

In simple terms, productivity is the measure of what a worker can produce working for one hour. However, the image that many people have that high productivity indicates an enthusiastic, energetic labor force and low productivity implies a lazy labor force is not generally correct. Better indicators of the productivity of the labor force are the efficiency of the equipment the workers operate and their training and education. Research on the growth of productivity in industrialized nations indicates that the larger the proportion of GDP a nation invests in capital goods, the higher will be its rate of productivity growth. The United States has been investing a smaller proportion of its GDP in capital goods than other western capital countries which undoubtedly has been a factor in our recent productivity slowdown.

Inflation and Productivity. One of the key factors in determining the level of inflation is the relationship between labor costs and productivity. Unit labor costs are equal to hourly compensation divided by output per unit of labor. There is a very close relationship between increases in prices and increases in unit labor costs because increases in prices must equal the growth in unit labor costs and unit profits. Wage increases unaccompanied by similar increases in productivity foster inflation. Productivity permits profits to rise and wages to climb without accompanying inflation. Stagnating productivity means that higher wages are translated into rising unit labor costs which stifles U.S. international competitiveness.

The Productivity Slowdown. From 1948–1973, growth of output per worker was 2.45%. From 1973–1982, this growth was virtually nil. Although productivity has improved since 1982, the growth rate is less than half the rate for the period 1948–1973. The slackening of U.S. productivity growth has had a dampening effect on the improvement in living standards. Why has productivity grown so much less after 1973? Although economists still debate the issue, several reasons can be offered:

1. The tremendous technological lead after World War II was largely dissipated by the 1970s. This process was largely inevitable as other countries recovered from the destructive effects of World War II.
2. An erosion of business profits occurred because of the slowdown in economic growth and an increase in the rate of inflation. The decline in profit rates reduced the incentive to invest as evidenced by the reduction in the growth rate of capital stock.
3. A large number of young employees and married women entered the labor force with little or no previous work experience. Their relative lack of experience also meant that they were relatively less productive.

Productivity in the 1990s. Many economists expect productivity to improve in the 1990s. Some of the factors they cite are the recent rapid growth in business investment in labor-saving capital equipment which should enhance productivity in the future, the increase in research and development spending as a percentage of gross domestic product, computerization and robotics, and a more mature and productive labor force with the end of the baby boom. Investors should watch the release of the quarterly figures to see if this prediction materializes. The 2.9% increase in 1992, following the flat performance in 1990 and the feeble increase of 0.5% in 1991, is encouraging. Only a 0.1% speedup in the annual rate of productivity growth can add more than $1 billion to the GDP. If productivity growth increases to its traditional historical rates, it enhances the prospect of strong economic growth and low inflation.

10

UNEMPLOYMENT STATISTICS

Unemployment can be divided into three basic types: frictional, structural, and cyclical. *Frictional unemployment* is short-term unemployment that results from such factors as individuals voluntarily switching jobs, fired employees seeking reemployment, employees seeking their first job, and the seasonal pattern of employment in such industries as construction and recreation.

Structural unemployment refers to long-term unemployment caused by changes in consumer demand and in technology. These types of changes cause some workers to become unemployed for long periods of time or permanently. Because of changes in the nature of the economy, the talents of some workers become obsolete. Structural unemployment is not caused by general business fluctuations nor does it involve the normal movement of workers from one job to another.

Cyclical unemployment refers to unemployment caused by business fluctuations. This results when the economy is in a recession or depression and aggregate demand is insufficient to maintain full employment. When the overall level of business activity decreases, cyclical unemployment increases. Conversely, when overall business activity picks up, cyclical unemployment drops. A prominent economist, Arthur Okun, quantified the relationship between unemployment and GDP. This relationship, called Okun's Law, indicates that the rate of unemployment declines by one percentage point for every two percentage points of increase in the rate of economic growth (GDP).

Full employment does not mean zero unemployment. Frictional and structural unemployment are unavoidable, thus the definition of full employment allows for less than

100% employment. One way to examine full employment is to note that it is achieved when cyclical unemployment is zero. But any definition of full employment is going to change as the demographics of the labor force change, institutional factors change, and the economy evolves.

Measuring Unemployment. The unemployment rate is reported on the first Friday of each month for the previous month. The data is collected by the Bureau of Labor Statistics, which conducts a nationwide random survey of 60,000 households per month. Despite the comprehensive nature of the sample and the sophisticated interviewing techniques used, the data collected has been subjected to criticism on several counts:

1. The official data regards part-time workers as fully employed. Many of these workers want full-time jobs but can't find them.
2. The data excludes the discouraged workers who have given up hope of finding employment. Only those unemployed workers who are actively seeking employment are classified as unemployed. Discouraged workers are classified as "not in the labor force."

As a result, the unemployment statistics underestimate the true extent of unemployment. Many economists estimate that the reported unemployment rate is 2–3% less than the true rate of unemployment.

Significance to Investors. One of the leading indicators used by economists to forecast future business activity is the average weekly claims for unemployment insurance. This indicator serves as a surrogate for the nation's unemployment rate. Economists have found this indicator to be extremely powerful in signaling future business activity.

A rough rule of thumb is that when unemployment claims are consistently less than 400,000 a week, the economy is said to be strengthening.

Analysts also use this indicator as a measure of the future course of general price levels. At higher levels of unemployment, increased economic activity is less likely to be accompanied by inflationary pressures. When the unemployment rate is low and the economy is strong, increased demand tends to bid up the prices of all resources, including labor, resulting in upward pressures on price levels.

Recent Changes. In early 1994, the Bureau of Labor Statistics will implement a major overhaul of its jobs survey. The questionnaire will be far more complex than the one the bureau has been using since the late 1960s. For one, it will give a more detailed picture of the U.S. labor force, thereby improving the understanding of trends in employment. Further, the new questionnaire will measure more accurately the number of discouraged workers.

11

GOVERNMENT DEFICITS

A budget deficit is the amount by which outlays or expenditures exceed receipts or revenues. Budget deficits have become routine for the federal government. For example, during 1992, the federal government had receipts of $1.092 trillion and expenditures of $1.382 trillion, resulting in a $290 billion deficit. Although there was much talk during the 1992 election about reducing the federal deficit, most economists forecast continued deficits in the future. These deficits have to be financed by incurring debt, which involves the payment of interest. As of 1993 the interest on the national debt represented the third largest outlay of the federal government, ranking after national defense and social security/medicare, with outlays exceeding $200 billion. The staggering size of the national debt has become a topic of great concern as reflected in the widespread coverage in the media. However, little consensus is evident as to its future impact on the U.S. economy.

If individuals continue to spend more money than they earn, eventually they will become bankrupt. Is the same fate a possibility for the federal government? For two principal reasons, the answer to this question is "no." The first point is that government debt need not be eliminated or reduced. When debt becomes due, the government typically issues new debt to pay off existing maturing debt.

The second point is the government's control over the printing presses. The government has the power to create new money to pay the principal and interest on debt. If this power is abused, however, runaway inflation will be the result.

Burden of the Debt. How burdensome is the debt? With per capita debt exceeding $15,000, are future generations being unfairly penalized? These questions can be addressed by noting who owns the debt. Surprisingly, about 85% of this debt is owned by U.S. citizens and institutions. In other words, the debt primarily consists of one group of Americans owing money to another group of Americans. Therefore, although the public debt is a liability of all Americans as tax-payers, 85% of it represents an asset to those Americans who are bondholders.

Only that portion of the debt that is held by citizens and institutions of foreign countries is a serious burden. The payment of principal and interest to foreign investors and institutions involves a transfer of resources overseas in contrast to the payments made to domestic investors. The current size of the debt is not as much of a concern as its continuing increase and the rising proportion of it that is owned by foreigners. (The percentage of the debt that is foreign owned was approximately 5% in 1960.) The larger the percentage of U.S. debt that is foreign owned, the greater the burden on the American economy. The interest payments made to foreign owners of government debt ultimately lead to a reduction in the real income of U.S. citizens.

The national debt may remain in perspective by examining past economic history and changes in the national debt over time. Comparing the national debt relative to gross domestic product (GDP) provides a basis for making some interesting comparisons. Although the debt ratio rose from 34% in 1980 to nearly 70% in 1992, the latter ratio was not inconsistent with past performance. In fact, the ratio was approximately the same ratio achieved during the Eisenhower administration in 1955. Furthermore, it pales in comparison with the ratios experienced during and just after World War II, when the total national debt reached a high of 127% of GDP in 1946. Therefore, the current debt ratio is in line with ratios experienced in the past.

Surprisingly, the national debt is consistent with that of other western economies as well as Japan. In fact, the U.S. ratio of debt to GDP is less than the ratio of Japan, Italy, and Canada. Furthermore, it is only slightly above that of France and Germany. These comparisons indicate that the size of the current national debt should not be viewed as an insoluble problem.

How Serious Is the Deficit? The answer to this question is not as simple as it appeared before the 1980s. Previously, accepted economic wisdom was that deficits created inflation. In the eight years of the Reagan administration the national debt doubled to approximately $2.6 trillion while inflation subsided—despite the dire predictions of many economists.

Many observers are concerned about the impact that deficit spending has on interest rates, particularly during periods of full employment. The sequence is as follows: a deficit forces the government to enter the money market for financing. The U.S. Treasury finances the deficit by selling government bonds to the public. The increased supply of government securities drives down the prices of all debt securities, which corresponds to a rise in interest rates. This process is usually called the "crowding out effect" because private borrowing is crowded out of the market by government borrowing. How serious has the crowding out effect been? Economists disagree. An important factor in the 1980s was the inflow of foreign funds, which helped to finance U.S. borrowing and to ease the upward pressure on interest rates. In the early 1990s, the weakness of our economy reduced the impact of the deficit on interest rates.

Deficits and the Stock Market. The potential effects of federal deficits on the stock market depend upon numerous factors. Perhaps the most important factor is the condition of the economy. Budget deficits are most likely to increase output (GDP) and corporate cash flows when the economy is in a recession. During such periods, higher deficits are likely to boost stock prices. When the economy is near full employment, however, the positive output effects are likely to be counterbalanced by higher interest rates and inflation, factors that generally cause a decline in stock prices.

12

BALANCE OF TRADE

The balance of merchandise trade is defined as the difference between the value of merchandise exports and the value of merchandise imports. A trade deficit results when the value of imports exceeds the value of exports. A trade surplus results when exports outvalue imports. The U.S. trade deficit has become a focus of media interest because the U.S. ran large trade deficits for all of the entire decade of the 1980s. In 1980, the merchandise trade deficit was $36 billion; by 1987, it had zoomed to $160 billion. Largely on the strength of U.S. exports, the deficit declined to $73.8 billion in 1991. The weak economies of our major trading partners slowed the increase in exports leading to a $96.14 billion deficit in 1992. The recent increase in the deficit from the 1991 low has many analysts forecasting the return to annual trade deficits of more than $100 billion. Japan, for one, continues to run huge surpluses. Our accumulated trade deficits now have made us by far the largest debtor nation in the world.

How does the United States finance deficits? It must either borrow from abroad or sell off assets to foreigners. It has principally been the purchase of American securities that has provided for the financing of the deficits. When foreigners sell more goods to the U.S. than they purchase from the U.S., they obtain the dollars to purchase American assets. Comparatively high interest rates and a reputation as a safe haven for investment create incentives for foreign investors.

Causes of the Trade Deficit. In the 30 years following World War II, world trade grew rapidly and the U.S. increasingly became integrated with the world economy. In those years, the U.S. usually ran a trade surplus, fueling American investment in foreign assets. In the late 1970s, the U.S.

started to run deficits because of dramatic increases in the cost of oil imports. These deficits were not deemed serious until 1982, when the value of the American dollar began to soar in world markets in response to a restrictive U.S. monetary policy intended to subdue inflation. The Federal Reserve hiked U.S. interest rates, making U.S. investments attractive to foreigners and increasing the demand for U.S. dollars. An inflating dollar meant that U.S. goods became more expensive compared to foreign goods.

In 1985 the dollar began to decline, and the burgeoning trade deficit began to level off and then decline. This decline continued until the deficit hit a low in 1991. But a slackening in the growth of U.S. exports and rising imports changed the deficit picture. In 1993, the deficit is forecast to exceed $100 billion.

Many economists state that progress in reducing the trade deficit depends on progress in reducing the U.S. budget deficit. A lower budget deficit would reduce domestic demand, freeing resources for exports and reducing the need for imports. Any perceived lack of progress toward reducing the budget deficit could cause investors to lose confidence in the nation's ability to solve this problem. This loss of confidence could lead to sharp downward pressure on the dollar and higher interest rates, as foreigners withdraw their funds from dollar-denominated assets. The rise in interest rates, along with inflationary pressures resulting from the declining dollar, could then weaken the U.S. economy.

13

FOREIGN EXCHANGE

The price at which one currency can be traded for another is the foreign exchange rate. For example, suppose the U.S. exchange rate for the Canadian dollar is $.78. This means that it takes $.78 of U.S. dollars to buy one Canadian dollar. An alternative interpretation is that it takes $1.28 Canadian dollars to buy one U.S. dollar.

The lower the cost of the Canadian dollar in terms of the U.S. dollar, the lower the foreign exchange rate, and vice versa. By the same token, the lower the dollar exchange rate, the cheaper Canadian goods are in the U.S. and the dearer U.S. goods are in Canada.

A foreign exchange rate is a price and, like most prices, is determined by the interaction of supply and demand. Shifts in supply and demand cause foreign exchange rates to change. These shifts can be caused by factors such as changes in tastes, inflation, income, interest rates, and political outlook, in addition to technological improvements, weather, wars, speculation, and so forth.

Fixed Versus Flexible Rates. Exchange rate movements are of special concern to governments because they affect the value of all goods and services traded internationally and, as a result, redistribute income across national boundaries. For many years a system of fixed exchange rates prevailed internationally. This system meant that governments intervened to prevent foreign exchange rates from changing. Adherents believed that reducing the uncertainty of exchange rates would stimulate international trade and investment. A system of relatively fixed exchange rates managed by the International Monetary Fund prevailed from the end of World War II until 1971, when the U.S. dollar was devalued. By 1973, fixed exchange rates were abandoned by most countries.

Currently, a system of managed floating exchange rates applies. Governments allow the forces of supply and demand to determine rates—within limits. They are willing to intervene in the market by buying and selling foreign currencies to offset abrupt changes and to curb undesirable speculation.

Foreign Exchange Quotations. Foreign exchange rates are widely reported in the financial press as in Exhibit 4. The table provides the rates expressed both as dollars per unit of foreign currency and as units of foreign currency per dollar. These rates apply to transactions among banks that involve amounts equal to or greater than $1 million. The rates for smaller transactions are less favorable.

Most international trade involves a delay between setting the price of a transaction and receiving payment. As a result, one of the parties to such a transaction will lose money if the exchange rate changes by the due date. This risk can be reduced by purchasing or selling foreign currency for future delivery at a specified exchange rate. Large transactions of this kind can be handled through banks in what is called the forward market. The 30, 90, and 180-day forward rates for various currencies are also reported in the table in Exhibit 4.

EXHIBIT 4

Exchange Rate Quotations

Wednesday, August 18, 1993

The New York foreign exchange selling rates below apply to trading among banks in amounts of $1 million and more, as quoted at 3 p.m. Eastern time by Bankers Trust Co., Telerate and other sources. Retail transactions provide fewer units of foreign currency per dollar.

Country	U.S. $ equiv.		Currency per U.S. $	
	Wed.	Tues.	Wed.	Tues.
Argentina (Peso)	1.01	1.01	.99	.99
Australia (Dollar)	.6761	.6730	1.4791	1.4859
Austria (Schilling)	.08460	.08395	11.82	11.91
Bahrain (Dinar)	2.6518	2.6518	.3771	.3771
Belgium (Franc)	.02818	.02792	35.49	35.81
Brazil (Cruzeiro real) .	.0124285	.0125897	80.46	79.43
Britain (Pound)	1.5165	1.4882	.6594	.6720
30-Day Forward	1.5129	1.4845	.6610	.6736
90-Day Forward	1.5064	1.4783	.6638	.6765
180-Day Forward	1.4993	1.4712	.6670	.6797
Canada (Dollar)	.7564	.7608	1.3220	1.3144
30-Day Forward	.7554	.7599	1.3238	1.3160
90-Day Forward	.7532	.7582	1.3277	1.3190
180-Day Forward	.7504	.7557	1.3327	1.3233
Czech. Rep. (Koruna)				
Commercial rate	.0344709	.0345185	29.0100	28.9700

Source: *The Wall Street Journal*

14

COMMON STOCK

Common stock represents fractional shares of ownership in a corporation. It has certain advantages that make it an attractive investment:

1. *Liquidity:* Common stocks traded on stock exchanges can be quickly bought or sold at prices that are quoted in the financial press.
2. *Dividends:* Dividends are important to investors who desire ever-increasing income.
3. *Capital appreciation:* Many investors are less interested in dividends than in seeing the price of their stock appreciate. The earnings not distributed to stockholders in dividends represent tax-deferred income. The reinvestment of profits should help the company earn greater profits in the future. Other things being equal, the greater the earnings or profits in the future, the more likely the stock is to appreciate in price. Furthermore, taxes are not paid on gains until the stock is sold.

Exhibit 5 provides a graphic presentation of the returns from investment in common stocks, long-term government bonds, and Treasury bills with a comparison of the increase in inflation over the 67-year period. Each of the series starts with a $1 investment in 1925. Notice that common stocks were the big winners over the period 1926–1992.

The evidence is compelling that in the long run investments in common stock have outperformed investments in other capital markets. Although investors in common stock, for instance, assume greater risk than those who invest in corporate bonds, clearly the returns in the long run have been greater. Note also that while investments in the stocks of smaller corporations are riskier, their returns have exceeded the returns on blue-chip stocks.

EXHIBIT 5

Basic Series: Summary Statistics of Total Annual Returns 1926–1992

Series	Geometric Mean	Arithmetic Mean	Standard Deviation	Distribution
Common Stocks	10.3%	12.4%	20.6%	
Small Company Stocks	12.2	17.6	35.0	
Long-Term Corporate Bonds	5.5	5.8	8.5	
Long-Term Government Bonds	4.8	5.2	8.6	
Intermediate-Term Government Bonds	5.2	5.3	5.6	
U.S. Treasury Bills	3.7	3.8	3.3	
Inflation	3.1	3.2	4.7	

-90%   0%   90%

Source: *Stocks, Bonds, Bills and Inflation: 1993 Yearbook*, Ibbotson Associates, Chicago, 1993

Finally, a caveat to investors: The returns from common stock investments listed in Exhibit 5 results from averaging the returns from many stocks. Poor choices of stocks can lead to losses even when the stock market is rising. Thus the successful investor must be willing to expend the time and effort to select quality stocks.

15

STOCK EXCHANGES

Common stocks are traded primarily on nine stock exchanges in the United States. The largest stock exchange is the New York Stock Exchange (NYSE), whose list includes 2100 companies with more than 121 billion shares issued and a market value of about $4 trillion. A smaller version of the NYSE is the American Stock Exchange (Amex), which is also located in Manhattan's financial district. These two are considered national exchanges. Common stock is also traded on seven major regional exchanges. The number of shares listed as well as the number of shares traded on the NYSE has increased steadily through the years. Prior to the 1960s, the average daily trading volume was less than 3 million shares. Daily volume averaged about 15 million shares during the first half of the 1970s and exceeded 30 million by the end of that decade. Volume has exploded during the 1980s with daily volume usually exceeding 100 million shares. On October 20, 1987, a record volume of 608,120,000 shares was traded on the NYSE. In the 1990s, volume continued to increase with the average in 1993 exceeding 200 million shares.

Trading volume on the Amex typically varies from 5% to 10% of that on the NYSE. The disparity between the activity on the two exchanges is greater when measured by the value of trading because the price of shares on the NYSE tends to be higher than that of shares on the Amex.

Originally, regional exchanges traded the securities of the companies located in their areas—thus the origin of the name. However, the development of rapid communication expanded their scope. As a result, some stocks on the NYSE and Amex are traded as well as local stocks. The largest of the regional exchanges is the Midwest Stock Exchange located in Chicago. Its trading activity now exceeds that of the Amex to make it the second largest organized stock exchange in the United States.

Role of the Specialist. Stock exchange specialists are the center of the auction market for stocks. Their role is critical in maintaining an orderly market for stocks. The specialist is a member of the exchange who has been assigned responsibility for about 15 different stocks. Currently, there are about 400 specialists on the NYSE.

In their effort to maintain fair and orderly markets in stocks assigned to them, specialists perform four distinct roles:

1. *Agents:* Specilists act as agent for other brokers on the floor
2. *Dealer:* Specialists are also required to act as dealers, risking their capital whenever a temporary imbalance between buy and sell orders exists in any of their assigned stocks.
3. *Auctioneer:* In addition to quoting the current bid and asked price to other brokers, they also evaluate the orders they hold and establish a fair market price for each assigned stock at the beginning of each trading day.
4. *Catalyst:* Finally, specialists are supposed to serve as the market's catalysts, ensuring that orders in their assigned stocks move smoothly.

The performance of the specialists on the exchange has been the source of great controversy. Many critics complain that specialists are more concerned with trading for their own accounts than with maintaining a fair and orderly market. Criticism was fueled by the "crash" on October 19, 1987, when trading in many stocks was halted. Currently, block trades involving large lots of stock are handled not by the specialists on the floor of the exchange but by a negotiated sale through brokerage houses or investment banks.

16

OVER-THE-COUNTER MARKET

The term over-the-counter (OTC) originated when securities were traded over the counters in stores of various dealers from their inventory of securities. Currently, however, the term is a totally inaccurate description of how securities are traded in this market. The OTC market does not have a centralized trading floor where all orders are processed like the NYSE and the Amex. Instead, trading is conducted through a computer-telephone network linking dealers across the country. These systems allow dealers to deal directly with one another and with customers.

Securities Traded. The OTC market is a huge market including nearly 40,000 securities. Although OTC stocks represent many smaller, unseasoned companies, the actual range of securities traded is much greater than assumed. There are several reasons why some securities are represented in the OTC market rather than being listed on one of the exchanges. Some securities issued by smaller companies cannot meet the more stringent requirements of the exchanges. Unseasoned issues of smaller companies typically are traded in the OTC market.

In other cases, firms choose to have their securities traded in the OTC market even though they could fulfill the requirements for listing on the exchanges. These companies may wish to avoid the financial disclosure and reporting requirements required by the exchanges. Many large financial institutions continue to prefer to trade their securities in the OTC market.

In 1971, the National Association of Securities Dealers (NASD)—the organization of security dealers that regulates the OTC markets—started providing stock price quotations through its National Association of Securities Dealers

Automatic Quotations (NASDAQ) system. This computerized communication network provides current bid and asked prices on over 5,000 securities. Through a terminal, a broker can instantly discover the bid and asked quotations of all dealers making a market in a stock. The broker can then contact the dealer offering the best price and negotiate a trade directly.

NASDAQ has been extremely successful. Its dollar trading volume makes it the third largest secondary securities market in the world, surpassed only by the dollar volume on the NYSE and the Tokyo Stock Exchange. The NASDAQ frequently has a share volume that exceeds the NYSE volume for the day.

Reading OTC Quotes. Two lists of NASDAQ securities are published in newspapers. The principal list is called NASDAQ National Market Issues, which includes more than half of the stocks in the NASDAQ system. Inclusion is based upon a company's financial performance and investor interest in the stock. This list (Exhibit 6) shows actual transaction prices, like those shown for exchange-traded issues. The information presented is the same as that for NYSE and Amex issues.

EXHIBIT 6

NASDAQ National Market Price Quotes

52 Weeks Hi	Lo	Stock	Sym	Div	Yld %	PE	Vol 100s	Hi	Lo	Close	Net Chg
13¼	9	MidMaineSv	MMSB	.28	2.9	12	1	9¾	9¾	9¾	– ¼
10¼	5¼	MidSouthIns	MIDS	.24	4.4	5	26	5½	5½	5½	– ½
22¼	13¼	MidStS&L	MSSL	.40	2.9	26	89	13⅞	13½	13¾	– ½
28½	25½	MidsexWtr	MSEX	1.78	6.8	12	6	27½	26¼	26¼	–1¼
44⅝	36⅝	Midlantc	MIDL	1.64	4.1	7	454	40	39⅝	40	+ ¼
6¼	3½	MidwComm	MCOM		...	22	53	6	5½	5½	– ⅜
s↑ 16¼	6½	MidSouth	MSRR		...	19	232	16½	15½	16½	+1
42½	26¼	MidwstFnl	MFGC	.80	1.9	12	9	42	41½	42	– ⅛
26	14¼	MdwGrnProd	MWGP	.60	2.4	14	106	25¼	25	25	– ⅛
25¼	19	MillerHrm	MLHR	.52	2.4	11	259	21⅞	21½	21½	– ⅛
26¾	13½	Millicom	MILL		...	...	302	24¾	24	24¼	...
10¾	5	Miltope	MILT		...	29	12	8⅛	7¾	7¾	– ½
10½	7¼	MilwIns	MILW		...	6	1	7⅞	7⅞	7⅞	+ ¼
49	35½	MineSftyAp	MNES	.64	1.3	13	349	48¾	47½	48¾	+ ¼
27	24	MinrNtl	MNBC	.92	3.8	...	8	24¼	24¼	24¼	...
13¾	2¾	Miniscrb	MINY		...	6	1400	4 1/16	3 15/16	3 15/16	–1/16
27⅞	11½	Minntnka	MINL		...	29	1482	27⅜	26¾	26⅞	– ⅜

Source: *The Wall Street Journal*

The other list covers issues that do not meet all the listing requirements (see Exhibit 7). Many of these smaller companies are eligible for the NASDAQ Small-Cap Issues list. Each one includes the company name, dividend (if any), volume, closing price, and net change based on the previous close.

EXHIBIT 7

NASDAQ Small-Cap Issues Quotes

Quotes at 4 p.m. Eastern Time
Wednesday, July 28, 1993

Issue	Div	Vol 100s	Last	Chg
A&A Fd g		131	$3^5/_{16}$	$+ ^3/_{16}$
AAON		1038	$1^3/_4$	$- ^1/_{16}$
ACS Ent		147	$23^3/_4$	...
ACTV		595	7	...
ADM Tr		35	$^{19}/_{32}$	$+ ^1/_{32}$
AFP		10	$^{13}/_{16}$	
AGBag		438	$1^{11}/_{16}$	$- ^5/_{32}$
AGP &Co		4	$2^5/_8$	$- ^1/_8$
APA		20	$2^3/_4$	$+ ^1/_8$
ASA Int		54	$2^7/_8$	$+ ^1/_{16}$
ATC Env		38	$6^1/_4$	$+ ^1/_8$
ATC		60	$^1/_2$	...
Abatix		20	$4^1/_8$	$+ ^1/_8$
AberRs		138	$2^{31}/_{32}$	$+ ^3/_{32}$
Abraxas		123	11	$+ ^1/_2$
AcrnVn		377	$2^1/_2$	$+ ^1/_4$
ActnPr		360	$3^5/_{16}$	$+ ^3/_{16}$
ActP wtA		4	$^3/_4$	$- ^1/_{16}$
Actrade		55	$2^5/_8$	$+ ^3/_{16}$
Admar		40	2	$+ ^3/_{16}$
AdvEnv		458	$1^1/_8$	...
AdvMam		381	$9^3/_4$	$- ^1/_4$
AdvMedP		119	$1^1/_2$	$- ^3/_{16}$
AdNMR		948	$3^3/_4$	$- ^3/_{16}$
A NMR wt		351	$3^1/_4$	$- ^3/_8$
AdNMR wtB		30	$1^1/_2$	$+ ^1/_8$
AdvanLfe		666	$1^{15}/_{32}$	$+ ^1/_{16}$
AdvTech		50	$^1/_4$	...
Aerial		104	$4^3/_4$	...
AerSyst		5	$^5/_{32}$	...
Agristr		130	$^3/_8$	...
AirCure		185	$4^3/_4$	$+ ^3/_8$
ArCur wt		91	$1^5/_{16}$	$+ ^3/_{32}$
AirInt		109	$^5/_8$	$- ^1/_{16}$
Airln wtA		16	$^3/_{32}$	...
AirInt pf.06e		324	$4^1/_8$	$+ ^1/_4$
Ajay		427	$^7/_{16}$	$- ^1/_{32}$
Alamar		39	$2^1/_2$	$- ^5/_8$
Alamr wt		45	$^3/_4$	...
Alanco		131	$5^5/_{16}$	$- ^7/_{16}$
AlskAp s		72	$3^1/_4$	$- ^1/_8$
Albara		63	1	...
AlbionBc		15	$10^1/_2$	...
Alcde pf		1	$2^3/_8$	$+ ^1/_8$
Alcolnt		209	$2^3/_{16}$	
Alden .05e		15	$4^5/_8$	$+ ^1/_4$
AllQuote		123	$3^7/_8$	...
AllQuo un		10	$5^5/_8$	...
AldCAdv		73	$3^3/_4$	$- ^1/_8$
AlphaSo		1738	$^5/_{32}$	$- ^1/_{32}$
AlterSal		12390	$2^1/_8$	$- ^5/_{16}$

Source: *The Wall Street Journal*

17

STOCK TABLES

Stock tables summarize trading activity in individual securities. For example, composite results of the previous day's trading in stocks listed on the New York Stock Exchange and on five regional exchanges are found in the NYSE Composite Transactions table (see Exhibit 8). This table is typically found in the financial dailies and, sometimes in abbreviated form, in local newspapers. It provides crucial information that should be evaluated before making a decision about investing in a stock.

The name of the company issuing the stock is given in the third column. Because of space considerations, abbreviations for company names are used. The majority of the securities listed refer to common stock.

The abbreviation "pf" indicates preferred stock. On the extreme left of some of the entries, abbreviations such as "s" are displayed. These abbreviations are explained in a section labeled "Explanatory Notes" located at the bottom of the page. For example, "s" denotes that a stock split or stock dividend of 25% or more occurred in the past 52 weeks. The explanatory notes apply to both NYSE and American Stock Exchange (Amex) listed issues and NASDAQ over-the-counter securities.

The first column in the table reports the highest price paid for the stock over the last 52 weeks, excluding the previous day's trading. The second column gives the lowest price paid over the last 52 weeks. The final four columns on the right give the high, low, and closing prices for the day and the net change from the previous day. A ↑ at the extreme left denotes that the price is the highest traded over the last 52 weeks, while a ↓ at the extreme left indicates a new low for the previous 52 weeks. Sometimes a U or (H) are used to designate new highs, a d or (b) for new lows. A separate

EXHIBIT 8

New York Stock Exchange Composite Transactions Table

52 Weeks					Yld		Vol				Net
Hi	Lo	Stock	Sym	Div	%	PE	100s	Hi	Lo	Close	Chg
57½	49¾	Goodrich pf		3.50	6.6	...	300	52¾	52¾	52¾	+ ¼
67¾	45	Goodyear	GT	1.80	3.8	8	1302	48⅜	47⅞	48	...
26⅝	15⅝	GordJewlry	GOR	.52	2.0	...	712	26¼	25¾	26	− ⅝
13⅜	9	Gottschks	GOT		...	17	20	10⅝	10½	10½	− ⅛
34	23½	GraceWR	GRA	1.40	4.3	13	2165	32⅞	32⅜	32⅝	− ⅜
s 22⅝	17⅞	Graco	GGG	.52	2.9	8	23	18⅜	18⅛	18⅛	...
67½	51¾	Grainger	GWW	.88	1.6	14	221	54⅜	54	54¼	− ⅛
14	8⅝	GtAmFstBk	GTA	.60	4.8	6	226	12⅝	12⅜	12⅜	− ¼
52	33¾	GtAtlPac	GAP	.60	1.2	15	291	49¾	49⅜	49¾	+ ¼
68	49⅝	GtLakesChm	GLK	.76	1.2	11	388	66½	65¼	65⅞	+ ⅝
40	25¾	GtNorIron	GNI	3.65e	9.6	12	12	38	37¼	38	+1
47⅜	35	GtNorNek	GNN	1.12	2.8	6	1237	40⅝	40⅛	40¼	...
17½	12⅝	GtWestFnl	GWF	.76	4.4	9	7598	17⅛	16¾	17⅛	+ ½

Source: *The Wall Street Journal*

table lists new highs and lows for each day of stocks listed on the exchange.

Other valuable information besides prices is reflected in the table. Column 5 labeled "Div" is the annual cash dividend based upon the rate of the last quarterly payout. Extra dividends or stock dividends are indicated by appropriate footnotes. The next column provides the yield percentage, which is determined by dividing the cash dividend by the closing price of the stock.

The P/E or Price-Earnings ratio is computed by dividing the latest closing price by the latest available earnings per share (EPS), based upon primary EPS for the most recent four quarters. The P/E ratio is one of the most widely used measures for evaluating the price of a stock. It cannot be used alone when making decisions but must be compared with the company's past P/E ratios and with the P/E ratios of similar companies. The P/E ratio is generally an indication of how fast the market expects the company's earnings to grow. The higher the P/E ratio, the greater the potential growth in earnings should be.

Many investors use the P/E ratio of the blue-chip Dow Jones Industrial Average (DJIA) as a standard of comparison.

Thus, if the DJIA has a P/E ratio of 10 and an individual stock has a P/E ratio of 8, earnings are considered to be underpriced when compared to the market.

Column 8 gives the number of shares traded in each stock, expressed in hundreds of shares. Thus, 75 means 7500 shares were traded that day. Transactions generally take place in units of 100 shares commonly called a "round lot." A "z" before the volume figure means that the number represents the exact number of shares traded. Thus, "z75" means 75 shares were traded, not 7500. When the number of shares traded is less than 100, it is commonly referred to as an "odd lot."

In *The Wall Street Journal* some of the quotations are boldfaced, which highlights those issues with price changes of 5% or more from their previous closing price. Underlined quotations indicate those stocks with large changes in volume compared with the issue's average trading volume. The underlined quotations are for the 40 largest volume percentage leaders on the NYSE and the NASDAQ System. On the Amex, it highlights the 20 largest volume percentage gainers. Both of these features alert investors to stocks that may be of interest.

Investor's Business Daily provides three key items in its stock tables not available in any other newspaper:

1. *EPS Rank* measures a company's earnings per share growth in the last five years and the stability of that growth.
2. *Rel Str:* stands for relative price strength and measures each stock's relative price change daily over the last 12 months compared to all other stocks in the table.
3. *Vol % Chg:* shows a stock's trading volume for that day in terms of its percentage change above or below the stock's average daily volume for the last 50 trading days.

18

MARKET AVERAGES AND INDEXES

Dow Jones Averages

The Dow Jones Industrial Average (DJIA) is the most widely followed stock market average. The index was first calculated by Charles Dow in 1884 by adding together the prices of 11 important stocks and dividing the total by 11. The average was broadened in 1928 to include 30 stocks and the composition of companies has been updated over the years. The corporations represented in the index have always been large "blue-chip" companies. The divisor is no longer equal to the number of stocks in the index because it has been changed frequently to compensate for stock splits, stock dividends, and other factors.

Although the DJIA continues to be the most publicized index, there are also Dow Jones indexes for 20 transportation-company stocks and 15 utility-company stocks, as well as a composite index of the 65 stocks in the three indexes. The names of the stocks included in the indexes are printed each Monday in *The Wall Street Journal.*

The Dow Jones stock averages are price weighted, meaning that the component stock prices are added together and the result is divided by another figure called the divisor. As a result, a high-priced stock has a greater effect on the index than a low-priced stock. In other words, a stock whose price is $100 per share is going to affect the index more than a stock whose price is $30. A significant fluctuation in the price of one or several of the stocks in the index can distort the average; however, over the long term the DJIA has been an effective indicator of the direction of the overall market.

Dow Jones publishes in *The Wall Street Journal* a series of group indexes covering nine sectors of the economy as well as an overall index. The industry groups currently include about 700 stocks. All industry groups together make up the Dow Jones Equity Market Index. The Dow Jones industry group indexes and the Equity Market Index are market weighted, in that both the price and number of shares outstanding enter into the computation. Use of this method means that stocks with big market capitalizations influence the indexes the most. Dow Jones has not given any exchange permission to use its averages as the basis of any options market. The Major Market Index (MMI) is designed to mimic the performance of the DJIA.

A widely publicized theory using the Dow Jones indexes is the Dow theory, which tries to predict reversals and trends in the market. Dow theorists seek to detect the primary trend in stock prices. Primary trends are the bear (declining) and bull (rising) markets. Secondary movements last only a few months and are usually called corrections. Most Dow theorists do not believe that the emergence of a new primary trend has occurred until a move in the Dow Jones Industrial Average is confirmed by a similar move in the Dow Jones Transportation Average. A primary trend is not confirmed until both Dow Jones indexes reach new highs or lows. If this event does not occur, the market will return to its former trading range. Although Dow theorists often disagree on when a true breakout has occurred, the theory does provide a commonsense approach to guiding investors in distinguishing between bull and bear markets.

Standard and Poor's Indexes

Standard & Poor's indexes are all market weighted. S & P has six weighted indexes:

1. S & P 500 Stock Index (also called the Composite Index);
2. S & P 400 Stock Index (also called the Industrials Index);
3. S & P 20 Transportation Stock Index;
4. S & P Utility Stock Index;
5. S & P 40 Financial Stock Index; and
6. S & P 400 Midcap Index.

All these indexes are assigned values of 10 for the base period of 1941–43.

The S & P 500 is, next to the DJIA, the most widely followed barometer of stock market movements. Originally it was computed with a sample of 233, but in 1957 it assumed a sample size of 500 stocks. On a daily basis its movement is more representative of the movement of the stock market as a whole because of its larger sample size and the fact that the index is market weighted. It is made up of 400 industrial, 20 transportation, 40 utility, and 40 financial stocks. The index consists primarily of NYSE listed companies with some Amex and OTC stocks (see Exhibit 9). The S & P 500 is the basis for the most widely traded index option (see Key 23).

NYSE Composite Index

The New York Stock Exchange introduced the NYSE Common Stock Index in 1966. This broad based index measures the changes in the aggregate market value of all NYSE common stocks. The market value of each stock is obtained by multiplying its price per share by the number of listed shares. The sum of the individual market shares, the aggregate market value, is then expressed relative to a base market value of $50—a figure approximating the average price of all common stocks on the base date of December 31, 1965. If the index stands at 200, that means the average value of all common stock listed on the NYSE on that date is four times as much as it was on December 31, 1965.

As shown in Exhibit 8, the NYSE also computes group indexes for industrials, utilities, transportation, and financial stocks. These indexes are computed in the same way as the NYSE Composite Index, although a smaller number of issues are included.

Other Indexes

The American Stock Exchange Market Value Index is computed in much the same way as the NYSE Index. It measures the performance of 800 issues on the Amex. The base value of 50 is based on the close of trading on August 31, 1973, when this index was first introduced.

EXHIBIT 9

Stock Market Indexes

STOCK MARKET DATA BANK · 8/18/93

MAJOR INDEXES

HIGH	LOW (†365 DAY)		CLOSE	NET CHG	% CHG	†365 DAY CHG	% CHG	FROM 12/31	% CHG
DOW JONES AVERAGES									
3604.86	3136.58	30 Industrials	3604.86 +	17.88	+ 0.50	+ 297.80	+ 9.00	+ 303.75	+ 9.20
1683.08	1204.40	20 Transportation	x1640.10 −	2.14	− 0.13	+ 382.05	+ 30.37	+ 190.89	+ 13.17
252.04	214.76	15 Utilities	251.05 +	0.26	+ 0.10	+ 30.84	+ 14.00	+ 30.03	+ 13.59
1338.43	1107.47	65 Composite	x1338.43 +	3.19	+ 0.24	+ 183.45	+ 15.88	+ 133.88	+ 11.11
433.29	380.79	Equity Mkt. Index	433.29 +	2.49	+ 0.58	+ 39.75	+ 10.10	+ /20.00	+ 4.84
NEW YORK STOCK EXCHANGE									
252.87	222.11	Composite	252.87 +	1.60	+ 0.64	+ 22.46	+ 9.75	+ 12.66	+ 5.27
303.91	273.18	Industrials	300.68 +	2.69	+ 0.90	+ 15.68	+ 5.50	+ 6.29	+ 2.14
237.32	198.98	Utilities	236.93 +	0.08	+ 0.03	+ 29.09	+ 14.00	+ 27.27	+ 13.01
252.79	182.66	Transportation	252.62 −	0.17	− 0.07	+ 61.68	+ 32.30	+ 37.90	+ 17.65
225.41	175.49	Finance	224.50 +	0.31	+ 0.14	+ 44.75	+ 24.90	+ 23.67	+ 11.79
STANDARD & POOR'S INDEXES									
456.33	402.66	500 Index	456.04 +	2.91	+ 0.64	+ 37.86	+ 9.05	+ 20.33	+ 4.67
524.99	471.36	Industrials	517.86 +	4.28	+ 0.83	+ 26.49	+ 5.39	+ 10.40	+ 2.05
405.65	307.94	Transportation	402.70 +	1.08	+ 0.27	+ 80.99	+ 25.17	+ 38.95	+ 10.71
180.15	148.88	Utilities	179.19 −	0.07	− 0.04	+ 20.81	+ 13.14	+ 20.73	+ 13.08
46.89	34.58	Financials	46.42 +	0.10	+ 0.22	+ 10.97	+ 30.94	+ 5.53	+ 13.52
172.37	140.50	400 MidCap	172.37 +	0.81	+ 0.47	+ 28.24	+ 19.59	+ 11.81	+ 7.36
NASDAQ									
734.83	554.22	Composite	734.83 +	3.82	+ 0.52	+ 167.22	+ 29.46	+ 57.88	+ 8.55
757.05	586.01	Industrials	752.43 +	5.59	+ 0.75	+ 152.44	+ 25.41	+ 27.49	+ 3.79
907.30	665.44	Insurance	905.85 −	0.18	− 0.02	+ 222.35	+ 32.53	+ 101.94	+ 12.68
658.59	451.08	Banks	658.59 +	1.42	+ 0.22	+ 194.33	+ 41.86	+ 125.66	+ 23.58
325.11	245.36	Nat. Mkt. Comp.	325.11 +	1.71	+ 0.53	+ 73.82	+ 29.38	+ 24.55	+ 8.17
303.87	234.80	Nat. Mkt. Indus.	301.13 +	2.28	+ 0.76	+ 60.75	+ 25.27	+ 9.73	+ 3.34
OTHERS									
446.63	364.85	Amex	446.63 +	3.97	+ 0.90	+ 60.74	+ 15.74	+ 47.40	+ 11.87
284.57	238.81	Value-Line(geom.)	284.57 +	1.72	+ 0.61	+ 36.36	+ 14.65	+ 17.89	+ 6.71
242.82	186.50	Russell 2000	242.82 +	1.57	+ 0.65	+ 51.28	+ 26.77	+ 21.81	+ 9.87
4537.23	3899.31	Wilshire 5000	4537.23 +	27.95	+ 0.62	+ 509.20	+ 12.64	+ 247.49	+ 5.77

†-Based on comparable trading day in preceding year.

Source: *The Wall Street Journal*

The OTC Index supplied by NASDAQ covers 5000 OTC stocks as well as several subcategories. It is also a market-weighted index. Two additional NASDAQ indexes cover only the more widely traded National Market Issues. NASDAQ also publishes several specialized group indexes covering specific industries.

The Wilshire 5000 Equity Index was first introduced in 1974 to meet the need for an index that reflects the performance of the organized exchanges as well as the OTC markets. This index of 5000 stocks is the broadest index and thus is the most representative of movements in the overall market. This index is calculated in the same manner as the S & P 500 and the NYSE Composite Indexes. Its base value is 1404.595, its value on December 31, 1980. In 1993, its high exceeded 4000 indicating that the stocks in the index had almost tripled in value in about twelve years.

19

BUYING AND SELLING STOCKS

Before buying and selling stock, it is necessary to establish an account with a broker. Brokers, also known as account executives or registered representatives, are required by law to carry out their clients' investment decisions efficiently and professionally. To select a broker, check with family and friends or a trusted banker, lawyer, or accountant. Like other professionals, some brokers service their customers better than others do. Before finally selecting a broker, arrange for a full interview to discuss the firm's procedures and rates and evaluate whether this broker can best fulfill your needs and objectives. In the interview, don't be afraid to ask hard questions; and if the answers are not satisfactory, shop elsewhere.

Brokers can be divided into two types: "discount" brokers and "full-service" brokers. Discount brokers usually limit their service to buying and selling securities for investors who know precisely what they want. Their function is not to give advice about the securities their clients are considering. As a result, their commission rates are generally less than half of those charged by full-service brokers.

Full-service brokers, such as Merrill Lynch, can provide information about the securities of companies. They generally maintain a research department which provides information to its brokers upon request. In addition, the research department issues recommendations about stocks it favors, and provides forecast of future market trends.

Opening an Account. Opening an account with a brokerage firm is not significantly different from opening a bank account. You will have to provide your name, address, occupation, social security number, citizenship, a suitable bank or financial reference, and an acknowledgment that the customer is of legal age. Most investors open "cash accounts" meaning that they will settle transactions promptly without credit. "Margin accounts" are used when the customer wishes to use borrowed funds to supplement the investors' own commitment. The investor makes only partial payment for the securities and borrows the rest from a broker. These accounts are better suited to more experienced investors prepared to assume additional risks.

Placing an Order. When you decide to buy or sell stock, you contact your broker and ask for a quote on your stock. The quote consists of two numbers telling you the highest price anyone currently is willing to pay and the lowest price at which anyone is willing to sell the stock. Several choices can be made. You might place either a "market order," the best available price your broker can obtain for you at that time or a "limit" order, where the stock is purchased only if the price drops to a specific level, or a "sell" only if it rises to a specific level. If a limit order is placed, it can apply for that day only or else be "open" or "good till canceled," which means that the order is applicable until executed or until you cancel it.

If your order involves exchange-listed stocks, it will probably enter an electronic pathway. New York Stock Exchange issues will generally be processed by a computer system called SuperDot that processes orders and reports back to the broker in an average of 22 seconds. On the day following the trade, the brokerage firm can send a written confirmation and bill to the client.

20

SHORT SALES

Most investors purchase stock with the expectation that a profit will be made from a rise in the price of the stock. However, investors have an alternative way of generating a profit when they believe that a stock is overpriced and expect it to decline in the future. The strategy adopted in this case is to sell the stock short. A short sale is the sale of a security that is not owned with the intention of repurchasing it later at a lower price. The investor borrows the security from another investor through a broker and sells it in the market. Subsequently, the investor will repurchase the security and return the security to the broker.

Most brokers will handle all arrangements on behalf of the investor. Usually a broker has other clients who own the security and are willing to loan shares.

An important aspect of a short sale order is that an investor does not receive the proceeds of the order at the time the trade is executed. In a short sale, the money is kept by the brokerage firm until the short is covered, that is, until the security is purchased and returned to the lender. Furthermore, to ensure that the short position will be covered, the broker requires the posting of collateral. Most short selling is done through margin accounts, in which case short sellers are required to have in their accounts the required percentage of the stock's price.

Reports on the total number of shares sold short of stocks listed on the New York and American stock exchanges and the NASDAQ over-the-counter market are printed soon after the middle of each month in the financial press. A large short position in a stock is not necessarily a bearish or pessimistic indicator, according to many analysts. In fact, technical analysts frequently regard a large short position as bullish. They theorize that a significant pent-up demand exists for the stock among the short sellers, who ultimately will have to purchase it to pay back their borrowed stock. In such a case, a sudden buying rush is possible if the stock's price increases and investors cover their shorts.

Specialist Short Sales. As part of their effort to maintain an orderly market, specialists regularly engage in short selling. However, they also have some discretion when they feel strongly about market changes. Technicians who want to follow the smart money attempt to determine what the specialist is doing and act accordingly. When this ratio is low, it is considered a sign that specialists are bullish and are attempting to avoid short selling. When the ratio surges, specialists are assumed to be bearish. Short sales by specialists are reported weekly in *The Wall Street Journal, Investor's Business Daily,* and *Barron's.*

Technical Points. Two technical points relevant to short sales are important. First, a short sale can only be made on an uptick. In other words, execution can occur only after an increase of 1/8 of a point or more in the security's price. This restriction was implemented to prevent traders from forcing a profit on a short sale by pushing the price down by continually selling short. In addition, a short seller is responsible for the dividends to the investor who loaned the stock. The purchaser of the stock sold short receives the dividend from the corporation. As a result, the short seller must pay the same amount to the investor who loaned the stock.

21

THE SECURITIES
AND EXCHANGE
COMMISSION

Prior to the Great Depression of the 1930s, the federal government did little to regulate the securities markets. However, the depression resulted in the virtual collapse of the securities markets, fostering widespread criticism of their operation. In an effort to restore confidence in their operation, Congress intervened and established the Securities and Exchange Commission (SEC) to administer federal laws that seek to provide protection for investors. The overriding purpose of these laws is to ensure the integrity of the securities markets by requiring full disclosure of material facts related to securities offered to the public for sale.

Securities Act of 1933. The Act provides for the regulation of the initial public distribution of a corporation's securities. The SEC requires a registration statement, which includes such information as:

1. Description of the registrant's properties and business;
2. Description of significant provisions of the security to be offered for sale and its relationship to the registrant's other capital securities;
3. Information about the management of the registrant; and
4. Financial statements certified by independent public accountants.

The SEC does not insure investors against losses. Nor does it prevent the sale of securities in risky, poorly managed, or unprofitable companies. Rather, registration with the SEC is designed to provide adequate and accurate disclosure of required material facts about the company and securities it proposes to sell. A portion of the information contained in the registration statement is included in a prospectus that is prepared for public distribution.

The Securities Exchange Act of 1934. The Act provides protection to investors by regulating the trading of securities of publicly-held companies in the secondary market. Continuous disclosure of company activities is required through annual, quarterly, and special reports. Form 10-K is the annual report, which contains a myriad of financial data in addition to nonfinancial information such as the names of the corporate officers and directors and the extent of their ownership. Form 10-Q is the quarterly report, which contains abbreviated financial and nonfinancial information. Form 8-K is a report of material events or corporate changes deemed of importance to the shareholders or to the SEC. All of these can be obtained from the company or from the SEC.

22

INSIDER TRADING

Insider trading abuses have received wide publicity in recent years. Michael Milken, for instance, was sentenced to prison and fined over $500 million. An insider is basically a person with access to significant information before it is released to the public. The SEC has been very active in pressing cases against insiders in an effort to prevent them from benefiting at the public's expense from information available only to them.

Insider Trading Sanctions Act of 1984. Insider trading sanctions are designed to prevent the misuse of confidential information not available to the general public. Examples of such misuse are buying and selling of securities based on nonpublic information or relaying the information to others so that they may buy or sell securities before this information is available to the public. The SEC has a broad definition of insiders, ranging from corporate directors, officers, and executives to clerks who photocopy confidential information. All insider trading is not illegal. The officers and directors of a company may buy and sell shares of that company as long as they do not do so on the basis of information that is concealed from the public. However, the SEC requires all these people as well as owners of more than 10% of a company's stock to file a report showing their holdings of the company's stock. Subsequently, they must file reports for any month where there was any change in those holdings. These insider reports are made public and are widely reported in the financial press. In addition, several newsletters use these reports as a primary basis for their recommendations.

Using the authority given it under the Securities Exchange Act of 1934, the SEC has brought numerous civil actions in federal court against persons accused of insider trading. In addition, the SEC has been a strong supporter of legislation to increase the penalties against those accused of insider trading. The Insider Trading Sanctions Act of 1984 allows the imposition of fines up to three times the profit gained by the use of insider information.

Using Insider Information. Every week the SEC compiles a list of stock purchases, sales, and exercises of options by corporate insiders. This information appears in the *SEC Official Summary of Security Transactions and Holdings.* This data is widely reported in the press and is published weekly in *The Wall Street Journal, Barron's,* and *Investor's Business Daily.* Although investors don't know the reasons for insider purchases or sales, they can still use this information as a timing signal. Several academic studies on insider trading have discovered that stocks insiders buy significantly outperform the general market. Martin Zweig, a prominent investment adviser, defines an insider-buy signal as indicated when three or more insiders buy stock within the latest three-month period, and none sells. Conversely, he defines an insider-sell signal as indicated when three or more insiders sell within the latest three months, and none buys.

Several newsletters not only follow individual insider transactions but also track total insider purchases versus insider sales as an indicator of future market performance. The greater the total of insider purchases versus insider sales, the more bullish these services are on the future course of the market. Conversely, they regard it as bearish when total insider sales increase dramatically compared to total insider purchases.

23

OPTIONS ON STOCKS

Trading volume in stock options has grown remarkably since the creation of the Chicago Board Options Exchange (CBOE) in 1973. The listed option has become a practical investment vehicle for institutions and individuals seeking profit or protection. The CBOE is the world's largest options marketplace and is the nation's second largest securities exchange. Options are also traded on the American, New York, Pacific, and Philadelphia stock exchanges. The CBOE trades options on stocks, on Standard & Poor's 100 and 500 market indexes, on U.S. Treasury bonds and notes, and on foreign currencies.

What Are Options? An option is a contract that provides to its holder (buyer) the right to purchase from or sell to the issuer (writer) a specified interest at a designated price called the exercise price (striking price) for a given period of time. Therefore, three conditions are specified in options contracts:

1. The property to be delivered.
2. The price of the property.
3. A specified time period during which the right held by the buyer can be exercised.

Options have standardized terms including the exercise price and the expiration time. This standardization makes it possible for buyers or writers of options to close out their positions by offsetting sales and purchases. By selling an option with the same terms as the one purchased, or buying an option with the same terms as the one sold, an investor can liquidate a position at any time.

Two types of option contracts exist—the *call option* and the *put option*. A call option gives the buyer the right to purchase a specified quantity of the underlying interest at a fixed price at any time during the life of the option. For example, an option to buy 100 shares of the common stock of XYZ Corporation at $50 until a specified day in September is an XYZ $50 September call. Alternatively, a put option gives the buyer the right to sell a specified quantity of the underlying interest at a fixed price at any time during the life of the option.

The last date on which the buyer is entitled to exercise an option is called the option exercise date. If an option has not been exercised prior to expiration, it ceases to exist. Note in Exhibit 10 that there are prices for different months. All CBOE stock options expire on the Saturday following the third Friday of the expiration month.

At any given time trading is conducted in the nearest three months of a cycle. In Exhibit 10, for instance, there is a Ford/Mar/60, a Ford/Jun/60, a Ford/Sep/60. When the Ford/Mar/60 options expire, a Ford/Dec/60 option would be added.

An in-the-money option is when the striking price of a call option is lower than the market value of the stock or the striking price of a put option is higher than the market price of the stock. An out-of-the money option is when the striking price of a call option is higher than the market price of a stock or the striking price of the put option is lower than the market value of the stock. An out-of-the-money option will have little, if any, value, just before the expiration date. However, an in-the-money option has financial value, and the investor must exercise or sell the option before it expires and becomes worthless.

Intrinsic and Time Value. The value of an option is often viewed as consisting of two components: intrinsic value and time value. Intrinsic value reflects the amount by which an option is in the money. For example, when the market price of XYZ stock is $56 per share, an XYZ 50 call has an intrinsic value of $6.

Time value reflects what the buyer is willing to pay for an option in anticipation of price changes prior to expiration. The time value of an option typically decreases as the option approaches expiration.

EXHIBIT 10

How to Read Options Quotations

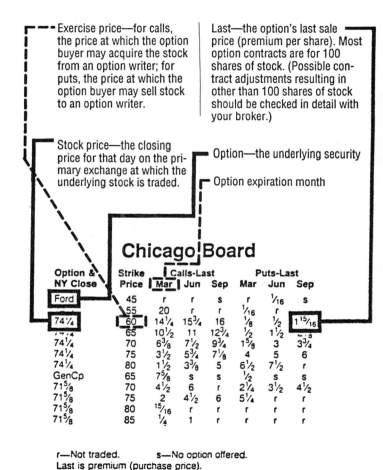

Exercise price—for calls, the price at which the option buyer may acquire the stock from an option writer; for puts, the price at which the option buyer may sell stock to an option writer.

Last—the option's last sale price (premium per share). Most option contracts are for 100 shares of stock. (Possible contract adjustments resulting in other than 100 shares of stock should be checked in detail with your broker.)

Stock price—the closing price for that day on the primary exchange at which the underlying stock is traded.

Option—the underlying security

Option expiration month

Chicago Board

Option & NY Close	Strike Price	Calls-Last			Puts-Last		
		Mar	Jun	Sep	Mar	Jun	Sep
Ford	45	r	r	s	r	1/16	s
	55	20	r	r	1/16	r	
74 1/4	60	14 1/4	15 3/4	16	1/8	1/2	1 15/16
74 1/4	65	10 1/2	11	12 3/4	1/2	1 1/2	2 5/8
74 1/4	70	6 3/8	7 1/2	9 3/4	1 5/8	3	3 3/4
74 1/4	75	3 1/2	5 3/4	7 1/8	4	5	6
74 1/4	80	1 1/2	3 3/8	5	6 1/2	7 1/2	r
GenCp	65	7 5/8	s	s	1/2	s	s
71 5/8	70	4 1/2	6	r	2 1/4	3 1/2	4 1/2
71 5/8	75	2	4 1/2	6	5 1/4	r	r
71 5/8	80	15/16	r	r	r	r	r
71 5/8	85	1/4	1	r	r	r	r

r—Not traded.   s—No option offered.
Last is premium (purchase price).

Source: *Understanding Options,* Chicago Board Options Exchange, Chicago Illinois, 1987, p.12.

Options Versus Stock. Options traded on exchanges such as the CBOE are similar in many respects to securities traded on other exchanges:

1. Options are listed securities.
2. Orders to trade options are conducted through brokers in the same manner as orders to buy and sell stock. Similarly to stock, orders on listed options are executed on the trading floor of a national exchange where trading is conducted in an auction market.
3. The price, volume, and other information about options is almost instantly available as it is for stock.

Differences between stock and options must also be recognized:

1. Unlike shares of common stock, there is no fixed number of options. The number of options depends upon the number of buyers and sellers.
2. Unlike stock, there are no certificates as evidence of ownership. Ownership of options is indicated by printed statements prepared by the involved brokerage firms.
3. An option is a wasting asset. If an option is not sold or exercised prior to expiration, it becomes worthless and the holder loses the full purchase price.

Who Should Buy Options? Options have some definite advantages. First, the maximum loss is limited to the premium paid for the option. In addition, options can produce quick profits with little capital. Finally, options are flexible and can be combined with other investments to protect positions and profits.

However, only investors with well-defined investment objectives and a plan for realizing these objectives should trade in options. Successful options traders must thoroughly research options, understand options strategies, and closely follow the options market on a day-to-day basis. Explanatory material on options trading is available from the CBOE, LaSalle at Van Buren, Chicago, IL 60605.

24

PREFERRED STOCK AND WARRANTS

Preferred stock is distinguished from common stock because it has certain preferential rights. Preferred stockholders have priority in the receipt of dividend income and claims on company assets in case of dissolution. The benefits of investing in preferred stock are similar to those of bonds. Preferred dividends usually are paid at a fixed rate. Most preferred dividends are cumulative, so that the omitted dividends are accumulated and paid in total before common stock dividends can be paid.

Unlike bonds, preferred stock has no maturity date—a specified date at which the initial investment will be returned. No such assurance is available with preferred stock. Market conditions determine the price an investor will receive upon sale.

Although preferred stock provides for reduced risks, its price typically has more modest growth potential than common stock. Preferred stocks that are not convertible into common stocks have little appeal to the individual investor. Investors should remember that if a company gets into financial difficulty, the interest due to bondholders takes precedence over the dividend claims of preferred stockholders.

Warrants. Warrants are options to buy a fixed number of common shares at a predetermined price during a specified time period. The definition is similar to that of a call option with some key differences. First, warrants are issued by the company that issued the stock rather than by an independent option writer. Second, the life of a warrant is usually much longer than the life of a call option. The typical term of warrants may vary from two years to perpetuity.

Warrants are usually issued by corporations as attachments to a new issue of bonds or preferred stock, to make the new issue easier to sell. When issued, the price at which the warrants can be exercised is fixed above the current market price of the stock.

For investors, warrants are pure speculations. Leverage works both ways. Warrant prices go up or down faster than the underlying stock. In this sense, they are similar to options. Their advantage over options is that the longer time to expiration gives the investor the opportunity to speculate on a company over a longer term.

25

FOREIGN SECURITIES

As the world economy becomes increasingly interdependent, many investors are now realizing the profits to be made by investing in foreign securities. With about 60% of the world's publicly traded stocks registered outside the U.S., opportunities abound for the investor willing to expend the time and effort in analyzing these markets. Returns on U.S. stock have lagged behind many of these markets since 1960. Non-U.S. markets as a whole have done better than the U.S. market in 17 of the past 26 calendar years (1968–1993).

An investment in a foreign stock can lead to a profit or loss in two ways:

1. The price of the stock in its local currency can advance or decline.
2. Relative to the U.S. dollar, the value of the foreign currency may rise or fall.

Of the several different methods for investing in foreign stock, the two most popular for individual investors are American Depository Receipts (ADRs) and mutual funds.

American Depository Receipts (ADRs). Individuals who wish to purchase specific foreign securities should purchase ADRs. ADRs are negotiable receipts representing ownership of stock in a foreign corporation traded on an exchange. ADRs are only issued on widely held and actively traded corporations. Furthermore, they are very liquid and have transaction costs comparable to U.S. stock. They are issued by an American bank and represent shares on deposit with the American bank's foreign office or custodian. ADRs allow investors to buy or sell foreign securities without actually taking physical possession of these securities. Purchase is made, and dividends are received, in U.S. dollars. Approximately

800 foreign corporations have ADRs listed against their securities, with the great majority traded in the over-the-counter market.

Mutual Funds. The easiest way to invest in foreign securities is to buy shares in one of the mutual funds that confines its investments to foreign securities. This course would be preferable for those investors who lack the time or inclination to investigate these markets closely. International stock funds offer the advantage of participation in a diversified portfolio of foreign stock as well as professional management. International funds are now available that specialize in particular regions, such as Asia, or specific countries such as Brazil or Germany. Prior to purchasing any of these funds, the investor should obtain a copy of the prospectus. A prospectus will describe the investment philosophy of the fund. (See next key for a fuller general explanation of mutual funds.)

26

MUTUAL FUNDS

For investors who lack the time or expertise to manage an investment portfolio, an excellent investment alternative is to purchase shares in mutual funds. A mutual fund is a pool of commingled funds contributed by many investors and managed by a professional fund adviser in exchange for a fee. Mutual funds are available to meet a wide range of investment objectives with nearly 2,000 funds currently serving the needs of investors. These varied needs are being met by the issuance of funds that specialize in municipal bonds, money markets, growth stocks, small company stocks, gold stocks, foreign stocks, and so forth.

In 1993, investors were pouring nearly $10 billion monthly into stock mutual funds. Mutual fund assets amounted to $2 trillion, compared to less than $50 billion in 1977. Mutual funds are considered the bank deposits of the 1990s. While the individual investor is reducing his or her direct holdings of stocks, indirect holdings are soaring. The percentage of stocks owned by individuals fell from 71% in 1980 to 49.7% in 1992, while the percentage of household assets in mutual funds jumped from 5% to more than 35% over the same period.

Types of Funds. Two basic types of funds exist: closed-end mutual funds and open-end mutual funds. A closed-end mutual fund is an investment company with a fixed number of shares that trade on an exchange or over-the-counter. Most of these stock funds trade for less than their net asset value.

Open-end mutual funds, by far the most popular type of mutual fund, are funds that issue or redeem shares at the net asset value of the portfolio. Unlike closed-end funds, the number of shares is not fixed but increases as investors purchase more shares. These shares are not traded on any market. Typically, large mutual fund organizations manage families of funds that may include, for example, one or more growth stock funds, gold funds, money market funds, bond funds, and small company stock funds. Usually an investor may switch from one fund to another within the same family of funds at no cost or for a small fee.

Open-end mutual funds can also be divided into load and no-load funds based upon whether they charge a sales fee when the fund is initially issued. A load fund is often sold by a stockbroker or financial adviser who charges a fee up to 8.5% of net asset value, which is deducted from the amount of the investment.

No-load funds are typically purchased directly from the fund without stockbroker involvement. There is no initial sales charge. Studies have found no evidence that load funds perform better than no-load funds.

Reading Mutual Fund Quotations. In 1993, *The Wall Street Journal* dramatically improved its mutual fund quotations so that they include details of each fund's performance, sales charge, annual fund expenses, and investment objective (see Exhibit 11). Funds are listed under the name of the sponsor such as AAL Mutual Funds. In the second column, funds are classified according to their investment objectives. A detailed explanation of these objectives can be found at the bottom of the page. The net asset value, or fund's share price (established the preceding trading day), is presented in the third column, and the net change from the previous day is shown in the fifth column. The fourth column displays the offering price, which is the per-share price including "load" or sales charge, or NL if the fund is "no load." The final columns present information on total return—price plus reinvested distributions—calculated for various time periods; year-to-date performance is shown daily. Each fund is ranked A, B, C, D, or E according to its performance relative to others with the same investment objective.

Selecting Mutual Funds. Before purchasing a mutual fund, an investor should check its performance record. *Barron's* publishes special mutual fund surveys quarterly in mid-February, May, August, and November, including articles and performance statistics. *Forbes'* highly regarded survey is published in August or September and features ten-year performance records of all funds, a selective "honor roll" of outstanding funds, and a ranking of how funds have performed in up and in down markets. In February of each year, *Business Week* publishes a scoreboard which assigns ratings to mutual funds that weigh five years of total returns against the amount of risk taken to make those returns. Finally, *Money* publishes regular articles about mutual funds and extensive quarterly statistics on performance.

EXHIBIT 11

Mutual Fund Price Quotations

Monday, April 17, 1989
Price ranges for Investment companies, as quoted by the National Association of Securities Dealers. NAV stands for net asset value per share; the offering includes net asset value plus maximum sales charge, if any.

	NAV	Offer NAV Price Chg.		NAV	Offer NAV Price Chg.
GwWsh p	12.91	13.59− .03	**MFS Lifetime:**		
Grth Ind	8.36	8.36+ .03	CapG †	10.43	10.43+ .01
Guardian Funds:			Globl †	11.25	11.25+ .08
Bond	11.39	NL.....	Sectr †	9.21	9.21+ .02
ParkA	22.78	23.85− .03	Emg †	6.75	6.75+ .02
Stock	21.17	NL+ .01	DivPl †	8.82	8.82+ .01
HTInseq	11.69	12.24− .01	GvPl †	7.64	7.64.....
HarbEq	12.18	NL− .01	Hilnc †	6.66	6.66.....
HarbrG	11.84	NL− .01	Intlnc †	9.49	9.49+ .01
Hart EGt	13.15	13.56− .04	MuBd †	8.18	8.18+ .01

Source: *The Wall Street Journal*

27

MONEY MARKET FUNDS

A safe place to park your savings is in money market mutual funds. Money funds are mutual funds that invest in short-term debt instruments. These include government securities, bank certificates of deposit and commercial paper (short-term corporate IOUs). Commercial paper typically composes half of a taxable money market fund's portfolio. Because money funds are required by the SEC to invest in debt instruments that mature in 90 days or less, there is relatively little risk of default on those loans.

Although money funds are designed to keep a stable share price of $1, the yield will vary as the general level of interest rates changes. Money funds often pay substantially more than a regular savings or checking account. In addition, you can usually earn about 1% more than by keeping your savings in a bank money market deposit account.

Although money funds are relatively safe, they are not entirely risk free. Unlike bank money market deposit accounts, which are federally insured up to $100,000, money funds are not insured. In the summer of 1990, several major funds suffered defaults on commercial paper they owned. The parent companies purchased the bad commercial paper so that the funds' share value would not drop below $1.

These events spurred the SEC and the industry's trade group, the Investment Company Institute (ICI) to back more stringent money fund safety regulations. Although these investments are not foolproof, no one has lost money in a true money fund. Those investors unwilling to assume any risk can still buy money funds that invest only in government securities such as Vanguard Money Market Trust Federal Portfolio (1-800-622-7447). Although you will have to sacrifice some yield in return for their greater safety, their return will still exceed that of most bank money market deposit accounts.

Some money funds pay significantly higher yields than others. Although you might assume that this difference is caused by the higher-yielding funds putting their investors' money into riskier securities, this may not be the case. The most significant factor causing the difference among funds is the management and operating fees they charge. According to Donoghue's Money Fund Report (1-800-343-5413), expense charges produce almost two-thirds of the variation in money fund yields.

The average money fund's expense ratio (annual expenses as a percentage of assets) is about 0.75%. This ratio indicates that a fund earning 5% in interest from its securities would yield a return to its investors of 4.25%. Expense charges can range as high as 1.5% to as low as about .33% at Vanguard. In other words, you could easily boost your return by more than half a percentage point by switching into funds with lower expenses.

Some funds have temporarily waived their fees altogether in order to attract new business. These special offers help new funds to grow rapidly. Large funds are desirable because fixed operating costs can be spread over a broader shareholder base, and the fund manager's personal return increases because it is typically set as a percentage of assets. You should be aware of when the fee waiver expires. Once the promotion ends, the manager's fee could sharply increase.

The dividends you earn on most money market funds are fully taxable. Those investors in a high tax bracket might find tax-exempt money funds attractive. Like all money funds they invest in short-term debt securities and their share prices remain at $1. But tax-free funds buy only municipal securities, which generally are exempt from federal tax.

Before investing in a tax-free money fund, you should calculate the taxable equivalent yield. This process involves two steps:

Step 1. Subtract your tax bracket from 1. Assuming you're in the 28% tax bracket, the answer would be 0.72.

Step 2. Divide the tax-free yield by the answer you got in Step 1, 0.72. If the tax-free yield is 3%, divide 3% by 0.72. The answer, 4.17%, is the taxable equivalent yield.

If you live in a state with high income taxes, you can further reduce taxes by investing in single-state tax-free funds. These funds let you skip state as well as federal taxes by investing only in securities issued by municipalities in one state. Most states exempt their residents from state income tax on municipal securities issued in that state. Therefore, the interest from single-state funds is free of state taxes as well as federal taxes for residents of that state. Moreover, if you live in a county or city that has an income tax, the interest is generally exempt from their local taxes.

Assets in this section of the mutual fund industry have mushroomed recently. Both *Money* and *The Wall Street Journal* regularly list these funds.

28

MUTUAL FUND PROSPECTUS

The prospectus is the single most important document produced by a mutual fund, and every investor should examine a prospectus before buying a mutual fund. Before a fund will accept your initial order, you must acknowledge that you are familiar with the prospectus. Further, current shareholders must receive new prospectuses when updated (at least once every fourteen months).

The prospectus is organized into sections, and it must cover certain specific topics. The descriptions can seem very technical, but there is good reason for this precision. The prospectus is an official document that requires SEC approval. The SEC has strict guidelines on what can be said in a prospectus and how information must be presented on past performance, expenses, and fees. But, the SEC's approval of a prospectus does not imply approval of any investment.

The cover of the prospectus usually gives a quick rundown of the fund, including its investment objectives, sales or redemption charges, minimum investment, retirement plans available, address, and phone number. The body of the prospectus provides a more detailed description.

Near the front is a table that describes all the expenses and fees. The table includes three sections. The first section describes maximum sales charges on purchases and reinvested dividends, deferred sales charges, redemption fees, and exchange fees.

Until the mid-1980s, mutual funds were split between the "loads" (which could charge up to 8.5%) and the "no-loads." A load is a sales commission that goes to whoever sells fund shares to an investor and does not go to anyone responsible for managing the fund's assets. If you invest $1,000 and pay a 5% load, only $950 of your money gets invested. If you purchased a no-load fund, the entire $1,000 is invested for you.

More recently, mutual fund companies have introduced a variety of fees and charges such as "contingent deferred sales charges" and "12b-1" fees. Contingent deferred sales charges are often called "exit fees" or "back-end loads."

To illustrate, a fund might charge you 5% of its value if sold within the first year. Each year thereafter your exit fee might drop by 1%. After six years, no redemption fee is charged.

The controversial 12b-1 charge, named for the SEC rule that allows funds to levy it, is meant to help defray marketing and distribution costs. Instead of paying this charge once when you buy the fund (front-end load), or when you sell it (back-end load), you pay this fee annually based upon the total net asset value of the mutual fund. Funds with 12b-1 plans can charge up to a maximum of .75% of assets per year, or $.75 per $100 of assets.

The second section of the table describes the annual operating expenses, expressed as a percentage of fund net asset value. These expenses include management fees, 12b-1 fees, and other expenses. All funds charge annual management fees, which generally range from .5–1.5% of net assets.

Beginning in May 1988, the SEC required mutual fund companies to show in a table how fees would affect a hypothetical $1,000 investment, assuming a 5% annual rate of return. This section also indicates the total dollar cost to the investor if his or her shares were to be redeemed at the end of one year, three years, five years, and ten years.

There is no evidence that funds with higher charges deliver better performance than those with reduced fees. Although the expense ratio is not the only thing to consider in buying a fund, it should certainly be a factor. Certainly, an expense ratio of more than 2% is excessive (the average for stock funds is about 1.4%).

One of the most important sections of the prospectus is the section containing condensed financial information, which provides statistics on per share income and capital changes. The per-share figures are shown for the life of the fund or ten years, whichever is less.

The per-share section summarizes fund financial activities for its fiscal year. The financial changes summarized include increases in net asset value due to dividend and interest payments received and capital gains from investment activity. Decreases in net asset value are caused by capital losses from investment activity, investment expenses, and payouts to fund shareholders in the form of distributions.

The last line in the per-share section will be the net asset value at the end of the year. The net asset value is calculated by dividing the total assets of the fund by the number of mutual shares outstanding.

The financial ratios at the bottom of the table are important indicators of fund strategy and performance. The expense ratio is the ratio shown in the fund expenses section of the prospectus. The ratio of net investment income to average net assets is similar to dividend yield for a stock and reflects the investment objective of the fund. Bond funds would typically have ratios that are more than twice those of stock funds.

The portfolio turnover rate is calculated by dividing the lower of purchases or sales by average net assets. It tells you how frequently securities are bought and sold by a fund. The higher the turnover, the greater the brokerage costs incurred by the fund. A 100% turnover rate means the securities in the portfolio have been held for an average of one year while a 50% turnover indicates that securities have been held for an average of two years. The average portfolio turnover rate for a mutual fund is about 100%.

Check to see if the portfolio turnover rate is consistent with the objective of the fund. Aggressive growth mutual funds typically will have higher portfolio turnover rates, while conservative funds would have lower portfolio turnover rates.

In addition, you would like to see a fairly consistent turnover rate over time. A consistent turnover rate is an indication that the portfolio manager is adhering to the investment objective of the fund.

The investment objective section of the prospectus describes the types of investments the fund will make and the amount, in percentage, of assets the fund will normally invest in certain types of investments. This section will indicate whether the fund is seeking capital appreciation or income. It will often include the investment philosophy of the portfolio manager, a description of how he or she selects securities, and the anticipated level of portfolio turnover.

The fund management section names the investment adviser and provides a schedule of compensation for the adviser. Most advisers are paid based upon a sliding scale that decreases as assets under management increase. If you want additional information about a fund's officers and directors, including a short biography, you can request what is called a statement of additional information from the mutual fund company. It provides details not included in your prospectus such as the name, occupation, and compensation of directors and officers.

Recent Changes. As of July 1, 1993, the SEC required certain changes in the prospectus that make it much easier to evaluate a mutual fund's performance. Funds now have to disclose each year's percentage gain or loss. Previously, you had to compute this amount. Even better, the SEC now requires funds to compare their performance with a broader stock- or bond-market index so you can see how your fund performed relative to the market.

Amazingly enough, prior to 1993 no information about who was primarily responsible for running the fund was disclosed. Now you know the name of that person unless a committee runs the fund. In addition, if the fund manager changes, that has to be disclosed in the next prospectus mailed to you. This information will enable you to determine if the current manager is responsible for the fund's recent record.

29

MARKET
EFFICIENCY

After the stock market crash of October 19, 1987, when the Dow-Jones Industrial Average plunged 508 points, articles in *Forbes, Fortune,* and *The Wall Street Journal* discussed the efficient market hypothesis (EMH) and the insight it offered into reasons for the decline. Although the EMH has been a topic of academic interest and debate for the past 30 years, it has only recently received the attention of the financial press. Market efficiency is a description of how prices in competitive markets react to new information. An efficient market is one in which prices adjust rapidly to new information and in which current prices fully reflect all available information. The adjustment in stock prices occurs so rapidly that an investor cannot use publicly available information to earn above-average profits. According to the EMH, market prices already reflect public information contained in balance sheets, income statements, dividend declarations, and so forth. Thus, fundamental analysis cannot produce investment recommendations to earn above-average profits. Nor is there much value in technical analysis.

Evidence. Although the EMH provides important lessons for investors, its adherents may overstate their case. Several points should be emphasized. First, although much empirical evidence supports the EMH, several strategies have been able to beat the market consistently, and thus are exceptions to the market's efficiency. A market, rather than being perfectly efficient or inefficient, is more or less efficient. Generally speaking, efficiency is a function of how closely a market is followed. The case for the efficiency of stock prices on the New York Stock Exchange (NYSE) is undoubtedly stronger than for those in the over-the-counter market because most of these latter stocks are not monitored as closely. Second, market efficiency varies depending upon the qualifications of investors. For the majority of investors, the market is an efficient mechanism. However, there are investors who do generate above-average returns on a consistent basis. This performance by a minority of investors should not obscure the fact that the performance of mutual funds and the recommendations of investment newsletters indicate that it is very difficult to earn above-average profits on a consistent basis. The EMH is therefore an aggregate concept applying to the majority of investors or to the market as a whole.

Lessons of the EMH. Although many analysts are dubious about the EMH, it does provide some important lessons that should be absorbed by all investors:

1. Tips are almost always of no value. The market processes new information very quickly.
2. A portfolio should not be churned. A strategy that involves frequent purchases and sales of stocks is likely to be a loser because the commission costs eat up any profits an investor might make.
3. It is not easy to beat the market. Only a minority of investors can consistently outperform the market. High returns can usually be achieved only through assuming greater risk. However, greater risk raises the possibility of increased losses as well as gains.

Evaluating the Stock Market. How can investors increase their chances of "beating" the market? One relatively simple yardstick can assist investors in evaluating the current state of the stock market. This simple measure would have shown that the market was overpriced before the October 1987 crash.

The Dividend-Yield Gauge takes the temperature of the stock market by dividing the aggregate per-share dividend of the S & P 500 stocks by the S & P 500 index. The number is published in Monday's *Wall Street Journal* and weekly in the statistics section of *Barron's*. A bearish signal is indicated when the S & P dividend yield falls below 3%. A strong buy signal occurs when the dividend yield is in the 5% to 6% range. In August 1987 the S & P dividend yield had fallen to 2.5%—the lowest in over 100 years.

30

SECURITIES ANALYSIS: FUNDAMENTAL

Fundamental analysis involves an estimate of a security's value, called intrinsic value, by evaluating the basic facts about the company that issues the security. Once the intrinsic value is determined, it is compared to the current market price. If the current market price is less than the intrinsic value, a buy recommendation is issued. Alternatively, if the current market price is greater than the intrinsic value, the recommendation is to sell the security.

Intrinsic Value. Intrinsic value is the price at which a security should sell under normal market conditions. This price is determined by evaluating such factors as net assets (assets minus liabilities), earnings, dividends, prospects of future earnings and dividends (or risk), and management capability. Critical to fundamental analysis is the evaluation of earnings, particularly future earnings. Most fundamental analysts cite the expectation of future earnings as the most important variable affecting security prices.

Intrinsic value will change as factors that affect stock prices (e.g., earnings, dividends) change. Likewise, stock prices will change as the economic prospects of a firm change. However, stock prices will fluctuate about the intrinsic value if it is accurately estimated. External factors such as pessimism or optimism may cause temporary gaps between the intrinsic value and actual price of a security. Fundamental analysts believe that they can exploit these gaps.

Most analysts on Wall Street are fundamental analysts. These analysts make recommendations in published reports which are easily obtainable from brokers. Many of these reports are collected and published in *The Wall Street*

Transcript—an expensive but useful publication available at many libraries and brokerage firms. An interesting observation is that there are many more buy recommendations than sell. Often when an analyst switches from a buy recommendation to hold, the message really is "Sell, but I'm afraid to say so because the company in question is a client."

Commonsense Style of Investing. Does each of us have knowledge even the experts on Wall Street don't have? Yes, says Peter Lynch, former portfolio manager of Fidelity Magellan, the largest of all mutual funds. In *One Up on Wall Street* (1989), Lynch advocates a commonsense, down-home style of investing. He thinks investors should concentrate on their own neighborhoods . . . on what they know better than anybody on Wall Street. Ordinary investors can sniff out trends and spot clues months or even years before Wall Street figures them out by being aware of new products that appeal to their families. For example, he cites how his wife, Carolyn, discovered L'Eggs pantyhose at the supermarket and persuaded Lynch to buy stock in the manufacturer, Hanes, which brought him huge profits.

His advice is to read the local newspaper for information about local firms. Look for want ads for new employees, for construction people to work on a new plant or facility. Ask locally about the company—its employees, calling or visiting the company, mining the local media for information. Don't be afraid to ask questions! After digging around, you should be able to deliver a brief monologue on why you think the stock is a winner. Says Lynch: "Once you are able to tell the story of a stock to your family, your friends, or the dog (and I don't mean a guy on the buy says Caesars World is a takeover), so that even a child could understand it, you have a proper grasp of the situation." Don't underestimate what knowledge of local companies can do for you. Atlanta is full of Coca-Cola millionaires, Rochester of Kodak & Haloid (Xerox) millionaires, Cincinnati of Procter & Gamble millionaires, and so on.

31

SECURITIES ANALYSIS: TECHNICAL

Technical analysis is the attempt to predict future stock price movements by analyzing the past sequence of stock prices. Technical analysts do not consider such factors as monetary and fiscal policies, political environment, industry trends, or company earnings in attempting to predict future stock prices. Their concern is with the historical movement of prices and the forces of supply and demand that affect prices. Technical analysis is frequently contrasted with fundamental analysis, which attempts to measure the intrinsic value of a security and places considerable reliance upon financial statements and economic trends.

The tools and techniques of technical analysis are endlessly varied. However, there seem to be certain procedures that, it is generally agreed, underlie technical analysis:

1. Market value is entirely determined by the interaction of demand and supply.
2. Both rational and irrational factors govern demand and supply.
3. Stock prices generally tend to move in trends that persist for significant periods of time.
4. Changes in trends are caused by the shift in demand and supply.
5. Chart patterns often tend to recur, and these recurring patterns can be used to forecast future prices.
6. Shifts in demand and supply can be detected in charts of stock prices.

Technical Indicators. As mentioned before, there are numerous rules and techniques used to predict prices.

Technical analysis can frequently be looked upon as an arcane art, and evaluating some of the tools is nearly impossible because the interpretation is so subjective. This section discusses several of the techniques that are widely publicized and can be interpreted objectively.

Advisory Service Sentiment. The poll of more than 100 stock market newsletters published by Investor's Intelligence (1-914-632-0422), categorizes the forecasts as bullish, bearish, or expecting a market correction. In the aggregate, forecasts of investment advisers tend to follow the market's trend rather than to anticipate a change in it. Therefore, when sentiment for a market move becomes strong in a particular direction, a contrary move in the market is expected. High bullish readings in this poll are usually indications of market tops, while low bullish readings are signs of market bottoms.

Advances Versus Declines. This vital technical tool is a measure of the number of securities that have advanced and the number of securities that have declined each day. Major newspapers publish these figures. The ratio of advances to declines provides a better indication of the trend of the overall market than an index like the Dow Jones Industrial Average (DJIA), which is composed of only thirty high-quality stocks. This measure of the breadth of the market is particularly important at peaks and troughs. Technicians believe that the market may be near its peak if the DJIA is increasing while the ratio of advances to declines is decreasing. The market may be nearing a trough when the DJIA is declining and the ratio of advances to declines is increasing.

Investment adviser Martin Zweig likes to track this ratio over a ten-day period. He has found that if advances lead declines by a ratio of two to one over such a span (a rare occurrence) and you invested at this time, you would have made abnormally large profits in the months that followed. Thus, momentum tends to be greatest at the beginning of bull markets.

Moving-Average Analysis. According to technicians, this analysis provides a way of detecting trends in stock prices. A moving average can be computed not only for stock averages and indexes but also for individual stocks simply by dropping the earliest number and adding in the most recent number.

For example, a 200-day moving average is calculated by adding the most recent day's price to the closing prices of the previous 199 days and dividing by 200. The computation of a moving average tends to eliminate the effect of short-term fluctuations and provides a standard against which to compare short-term fluctuations. For example, technicians consider a downward penetration through a moving-average line as a signal to sell, particularly when a moving-average price is flattening out. On the other hand, analysts are bullish about a stock when the graph of a moving-average price flattens out and the stock's price rises through the moving average.

Locating Data. Data for technical analysis is available in both *The Wall Street Journal* and *Investor's Business Daily.* However, an additional source of invaluable information to technical analysts is *Barron's,* a financial weekly of about 150 pages that provides excellent general articles, a review of the past week on the financial markets, and about 80 pages of statistics. Included in the statistics is a section called Market Laboratory, which provides a gold mine of information for technical analysis. Subscribers should ask for a copy of the educational edition, which includes an article by Martin Zweig and Victor Hillery on how to use the Market Laboratory statistics.

32

ADVISORY
SERVICES

It is estimated that there may be as many as 500 investment newsletters with annual subscription prices ranging from $25 to over $1000 and a total of about a million subscribers. In their ads, these services often make extravagant claims about the value of their investment advice. Investors should be skeptical about the claims of omniscience on the part of these newsletters. The performance of many of these newsletters can vary dramatically from one year to the next.

Some market gurus can temporarily influence the price of a stock or even of the market as a whole. Joseph Granville flashed a sell-out signal early in January 1981 and was credited with causing U.S. stocks to lose $38 billion in market value the following day, with volume rocketing to a then record 93 million shares. Unfortunately, for Granville, he continued to be bearish and fell out of favor when the market turned upward in 1982.

Then 1987 was the year of Bob Prechter and the Elliott wave theory, an esoteric technical theory only its adherents fully grasp. He had predicted a bull market for the late 1980s, and when it occurred, many people thought he was the new financial demigod. However, his prediction of a bear market in the early 1990s has dimmed his reputation. In the future, expect new soothsayers to become fashionable.

Many newsletters use a primarily technical approach to evaluate both the market and individual stocks. Others take a fundamental approach including three of the largest: the *Value Line Investment Survey,* Standard & Poor's *The Outlook,* and *United Business & Investment Report.* Specialized services are also available devoted to options, futures, stock charts, small company stocks, foreign investments, and insider trading.

Evaluating Newsletters. Keep in mind that from year to year the performance success of all newsletters changes. A proper evaluation requires at least a five-year track record. Before purchasing a newsletter, investors might refer to *The Hulbert Guide to Financial Newsletters* published in February of each year by Mark Hulbert (703-683-5905), which tracks the performance of more than 100 newsletters. In addition, he publishes a newsletter devoted to appraising the newsletter industry entitled the *Hulbert Financial Digest* and writes a regular column for *Forbes.*

The cheapest way of sampling a variety of services is to write for the free catalogue published by Select Information Exchange, 2095 Broadway, New York, N.Y. 10023. The catalogue describes hundreds of services and offers you trial subscriptions to twenty services of your choice for a nominal amount.

33

TREASURY SECURITIES

The largest fixed-income market is that for U.S. Treasury obligations. These are backed by the full faith and credit of the U.S. government and, therefore, offer the investor maximum safety of principal and a guaranteed yield. Although the yield is typically less than on a corporate bond, Treasury securities are the closest approximations to risk-free investments.

The three most popular Treasury securities for individual investors are Treasury bills, Treasury notes, and Treasury bonds. Treasury bills have maturities up to and including one year. Treasury notes mature in between one and ten years while Treasury bonds range in maturity from ten to thirty years.

Treasury Bills. T-bills are most commonly offered by the Treasury with maturities of three or six months. These securities are issued every Monday in minimum denominations of $10,000 and in increments of $5,000 above the minimum. Investors bid for them at a discount by offering, for example, $99 for every $100 of T-bills. At maturity, the investor will receive $100. Yields are expressed on an annual basis, so that in the case of a three-month T-bill purchased for $99, the yield would be the discount of $1 divided by the price of $99 and multiplied by four because there are four three-month periods in a year. For this example, the yield would be 4.08%. The gain of $1 is interest income and subject to federal income tax but is exempt from state and local taxes.

Treasury Notes. T-notes mature between one and ten years. They are issued in $1,000 and $5,000 denominations with a fixed interest rate determined by the coupon rate specified in the note. The interest earned is paid semiannually and is exempt from state and local taxes.

T-notes have several characteristics that account for their increasing popularity. One is the low $1,000 minimum. Another plus is that their longer maturities usually mean a greater return for investors than T-bills can provide.

Treasury Bonds. T-bonds make up the smallest segment of the federal debt. These bonds mature and repay their face value within a period of ten to thirty years from the date of issue. They are issued in denominations of $1,000, $5,000, $10,000, $50,000, $100,000, and $1 million. A fixed rate of interest is paid semiannually, and the interest earned is exempt from state and local taxes. Some of these issues are callable or redeemable prior to maturity. A callable bond is indicated in the newspaper by a hyphen between the call date and the maturity date. For instance, if 1995-99 is listed under "maturity," that means the bond can be redeemed at any time starting in 1995.

Reading the Quotes. Exhibit 12 gives an illustration of how T-bonds, T-notes, and T-bills are reported in *The Wall Street Journal.* The price quotations for T-bonds and T-notes are given per hundred dollars of face value. The first column shows the original interest rate, the second column the month of maturity. In Wall Street shorthand, 10% bonds due in 1995 are called "tens of ninety-five." The third column indicates the year of maturity. The list is chronological.

Bid means the mid-afternoon bid price dealers were willing to pay that day. The asked price indicates the dealer selling price. The next column gives the changes in the bid price from the day before. The last column gives the yield or effective return on the investment.

In the bond market, a price of 100 is called par or face value, and each one-hundredth of par is called a point. The minimum price fluctuation is usually $1/32$ of a point, called a tick. To avoid the constant repetition of the number 32, a convention in the bond market prevails that figures after a decimal point or hyphen in a price represents 32nds. As a result, a quotation of 95-8 means 95 and $8/32$, or $95 1/4$.

In the T-bill section, the date under maturity indicates when the bills are to be retired. Under the bid and asked columns, the decimal takes on its customary meaning: 2.90

EXHIBIT 12

Price Quotations for U.S. Treasury Bills, Bonds, and Notes

Thursday, December 2, 1993

Representative Over-the-Counter quotations based on transactions of $1 million or more.

Treasury bond, note and bill quotes are as of mid-afternoon. Colons in bid-and-asked quotes represent 32nds; 101:01 means 101 1/32. Net changes in 32nds. n-Treasury note. Treasury bill quotes in hundredths, quoted on terms of a rate of discount. Days to maturity calculated from settlement date. All yields are to maturity and based on the asked quote. Latest 13-week and 26-week bills are boldfaced. For bonds callable prior to maturity, yields are computed to the earliest call date for issues quoted above par and to the maturity date for issues quoted below par. *-When issued.

Source: Federal Reserve Bank of New York.

U.S. Treasury strips as of 3 p.m. Eastern time, also based on transactions of $1 million or more. Colons in bid-and-asked quotes represent 32nds; 101:01 means 101 1/32. Net changes in 32nds. Yields calculated on the asked quotation. ci-stripped coupon interest. bp-Treasury bond, stripped principal. np-Treasury note, stripped principal. For bonds callable prior to maturity, yields are computed to the earliest call date for issues quoted above par and to the maturity date for issues quoted below par.

Source: Bear, Stearns & Co. via Street Software Technology Inc.

GOVT. BONDS & NOTES

Rate	Maturity Mo/Yr	Bid	Asked	Chg.	Ask Yld.
5	Dec 93n	100:04	100:06	....	2.19
7⁵/₈	Dec 93n	100:10	100:12	− 1	2.03
7	Jan 94n	100:13	100:15	....	2.60
4⁷/₈	Jan 94n	100:08	100:10	....	2.77
6⁷/₈	Feb 94n	100:22	100:24	− 1	2.90
8⁷/₈	Feb 94n	101:03	101:05	....	2.77
9	Feb 94	101:04	101:06	− 1	2.74
5³/₈	Feb 94n	100:17	100:19	....	2.76
5³/₄	Mar 94n	100:25	100:27	....	3.02
8¹/₂	Mar 94n	101:21	101:23	− 1	2.96
7	Apr 94n	101:10	101:12	− 1	3.08
5³/₈	Apr 94n	100:26	100:28	....	3.15
7	May 94n	101:19	101:21	....	3.19
9¹/₂	May 94n	102:22	102:24	− 1	3.17
13¹/₈	May 94n	104:12	104:14	− 1	2.93
5¹/₈	May 94n	100:27	100:29	....	3.22
5	Jun 94n	100:28	100:30	....	3.32

Rate	Maturity Mo/Yr	Bid	Asked	Chg.	Ask Yld.
8	Aug 99n	113:08	113:10	+ 1	5.26
6	Oct 99n	103:11	103:13	+ 1	5.32
7⁷/₈	Nov 99n	112:26	112:28	....	5.32
6³/₈	Jan 00n	105:05	105:07	+ 4	5.36
7⁷/₈	Feb 95-00	104:15	104:19	+ 1	3.90
8¹/₂	Feb 00n	116:09	116:11	+ 1	5.36
5¹/₂	Apr 00n	100:26	100:28	....	5.34
8⁷/₈	May 00n	118:20	118:22	+ 2	5.40
8³/₈	Aug 95-00	106:19	106:23	+ 2	4.22
8³/₄	Aug 00n	118:07	118:09	+ 2	5.45
8¹/₂	Nov 00n	117:02	117:04	+ 1	5.50
7³/₄	Feb 01n	112:30	113:00	+ 1	5.53
11³/₄	Feb 01	136:20	136:24	+ 3	5.50
8	May 01n	114:21	114:23	+ 3	5.56
13¹/₈	May 01	145:25	145:29	+ 2	5.52
7⁷/₈	Aug 01n	114:01	114:03	+ 2	5.60
8	Aug 96-01	108:10	108:14	− 1	4.63
13³/₈	Aug 01	148:10	148:14	+ 2	5.55

TREASURY BILLS

Maturity	Days to Mat.	Bid	Asked	Chg.	Ask Yld.
Dec 09 '93	3	2.85	2.75	....	2.79
Dec 16 '93	10	2.97	2.87	− 0.03	2.91
Dec 23 '93	17	2.83	2.73	− 0.03	2.77
Dec 30 '93	24	2.79	2.69	+ 0.02	2.73
Jan 06 '94	31	2.92	2.88	− 0.02	2.93
Jan 13 '94	38	3.02	2.98	....	3.03
Jan 20 '94	45	3.07	3.03	....	3.08
Jan 27 '94	52	3.06	3.02	....	3.08
Feb 03 '94	59	3.08	3.06	− 0.01	3.12
Feb 10 '94	66	3.11	3.09	+ 0.01	3.15
Feb 17 '94	73	3.11	3.09	....	3.15
Feb 24 '94	80	3.11	3.09	− 0.01	3.15
Mar 03 '94	87	3.11	3.09	− 0.01	3.16

Source: *The Wall Street Journal*

means 2 and $9/10$. The yield column represents the effective total return, and is used for comparison with other investments.

Treasury securities can be purchased directly from Federal Reserve banks by setting up a "Treasury Direct Account," which will link up with a checking or savings account at your bank into which payments from your Treasury investments will be automatically deposited. There are no fees. The alternative is to purchase the securities through a bank or brokerage firm, where you will be charged a small commission. You can obtain more specific information by telephoning the Federal Reserve Bank in your district. Offices are located in Boston, New York, Philadelphia, Cleveland, Richmond, Atlanta, Chicago, St. Louis, Minneapolis, Kansas City, Dallas, and San Francisco.

Significance of Interest Rates. The huge volume of T-bills makes them the most important short-term investment. Their yield has become the bellwether indicator of short-term interest rates, just as the yield on T-bonds is the bellwether for long-term interest rates. The size of this market, the creditworthiness of the federal government, and the popularity of these securities with institutional and foreign investors make Treasury interest rates extremely responsive to changes in economic conditions. In addition, the Fed buys and sells these securities to control the money supply and influence interest rates. As a result, changes in the interest rates paid by the U.S. Treasury affect the interest rates paid by borrowers in North America and around the world.

34

CORPORATE
BONDS

Corporate bonds are debt obligations that are secured by specified assets or a promise to pay. In effect, a bond investor lends money to the bond issuer. In return, the issuer promises to pay interest and to repay the principal at maturity.

Many new corporate bond issues with a variety of maturities are ordinarily sold each week. Some of these issues have maturities of approximately a year, while others have maturity lengths of thirty years, or more. In 1993, Disney startled the financial world by selling bonds that mature in 100 years.

Because bondholders are creditors, they have a prior claim on the earnings and assets of the issuing corporation, ranking ahead of preferred and common stockholders. Interest must first be paid to the bondholders before dividends can be distributed to stockholders. In case of dissolution or bankruptcy, bondholders have a prior claim on assets over stockholders. Only corporations in extreme financial difficulty will fail to pay the interest on their bonds.

Corporate bonds are typically issued in denominations of $1,000, called the face, par, or maturity value. If an investor buys five bonds, the total face value is $5000, which means the corporation promises to repay $5000 when the bonds mature. In addition, the corporation promises to pay interest, generally semiannually at a specified annual rate on the face value. The interest rate is commonly called the coupon or stated rate.

Bonds fluctuate in price, with market value largely determined by changes in interest rates. As the general level of interest rates rise, bond prices go down. Alternatively, as interest rates decline, bond prices increase. Other factors, such as the bond's rating, explained below, also influence price.

Understanding the different definitions of yield is critical to understanding bond pricing. *Coupon yield* is the interest rate stated on the bond. *Current yield* is obtained by dividing the stated interest rate by the latest price. The *yield to maturity* is the most important concept of yield because it is the yield upon which all bond prices are based. It includes both interest and the appreciation to face value at maturity when the bonds are bought at a discount or depreciation to face value when the bonds are bought at a premium.

Bond Ratings. One of the important factors in determining the interest rate a bond must pay to attract investors is the credit quality of the bond. The two most important companies evaluating bonds, Moody's Investors Service and Standard & Poor's, generally reach the same conclusions about each bond. Exhibit 13 provides the risk classifications and a general description of their meaning. Bonds rated AAA by Standard & Poor's or Aaa by Moody's are the highest-grade obligations, meaning they possess the ultimate degree of protection as to principal and interest. Bonds rated below BBB or Baa are speulative in nature and are called junk bonds. These lower-quality bonds must pay higher yields in order to attract investors.

Reading the Quotes. A typical listing from *The Wall Street Journal* will look as follows:

Bonds	Cur Yld	Vol	Close	Net Chg
Mobil 8 3/8 01	7.4	25	112 1/2	+ 1/2

The first column shows the name of the issuer. The second column notes the original interest rate (coupon rate) and the year of maturity. Thus, 8 3/8 01 is interpreted as 8 3/8% bonds due in 2001. The third column gives the current yield, or the interest obtained by dividing the original interest rate by the latest price. In this case, each bond pays $83.75 annual interest, so the current yield is 7.4%. The fourth column indicates the volume of trading, in thousands of dollars. In this case, $25,000 was traded. The last two columns provide the closing price and the change from the previous day, which is an increase of $.50 per bond.

Bond prices are quoted as a percentage of face value. In our example, the closing price of 112 1/2 means that the

EXHIBIT 13

Bond Ratings

Description	Moody's	Standard & Poor's
High Grade	Aaa	AAA
	Aa	AA
Medium Grade	A	A
	Baa	BBB
Speculative	Ba	BB
	B	B
Default	Caa	CCC
	Ca	CC
	C	C

actual price of the bond is $112^{1}/_{2} \times \$1000$ face value = $1125 for each bond. In discussion of bonds, the term "basis point" is often used. A basis point is $^{1}/_{100}$th of one percent and is a convenient way to discuss changes in yields. For example, an increase in yield from 9.5% to 10% is a 50 basis point increase.

Junk Bonds. Many investors interested in higher yields are purchasing so-called junk bonds—those below investment grade—that yield substantially more than higher quality bonds but also carry greater risk. Investment grade denotes obligations that are eligible for investment by various institutions such as banks, insurance companies, and savings & loan associations.

Junk bonds are a mature $200 billion market that is here to stay. It provides firms with a way to raise sorely needed capital. Most investors should invest in junk bonds only through a mutual fund, where risk is diversified by having a large number of junk bonds in the portfolio.

35

MUNICIPAL BONDS

Municipal bonds are debt securities issued by state and local governments and local government agencies and authorities. Municipal bonds differ from corporate bonds in three significant respects:

1. The interest on municipal bonds is exempt from federal income taxes. In addition, if these bonds are issued in the investor's state of residency, they are also exempt from state and local income taxes. This tax-exempt feature is what makes municipal bonds or "munis" attractive to investors in higher income tax brackets.

2. Most municipal bond issues are serial bond issues as opposed to the term maturities of corporate and Treasury bonds. A serial bond issue involves a series of maturity dates. The advantage of having a portion of the bonds mature periodically over the life of the issue is that it spreads fixed principal repayment obligations over a number of years to correspond to the flow of tax revenue receipts.

3. Most municipal bonds are issued in $5,000 denominations while corporate bonds are issued in $1,000 denominations.

Types of Municipal Bond Issues. Two general types of munis exist: general obligation bonds and revenue bonds. General obligation bonds (GO's) are backed by the full taxing power of the issuer, thus they are considered the safest munis.

Revenue bonds are payable from the revenues generated by a particular project such as a sewer, gas or electric system, airport, or toll bridge financed by the issue. Because only these revenues are pledged to pay interest and repay the principal, revenue bonds are generally considered to possess higher default risk than GO's. As a consequence, they usually carry higher yields.

Selecting Municipal Bonds. Standard & Poor's Corporation and Moody's Investors Service are the two major municipal rating agencies. In general, the higher the safety rating the lower the interest, although other factors in addition to rating also affect a bond's price. The symbols used by Moody's and Standard & Poor's are the same symbols used in rating corporate bonds.

For those investors with limited time and resources, the best way to invest in munis is to purchase municipal bond mutual funds. This approach affords the investor diversification as well as constant supervision by professional management. The minimum required investment is usually $1,000.

Price Quotations. The market for municipal bonds is not as liquid as the market for federal government securities. Trading is not very active because many of these securities are not issued in large amounts. As a result, the spread between bid and asked prices in this market tends to be larger than for similar federal government issues. Prices on municipal bonds are seldom reported in local newspapers. *The Wall Street Journal* and some other large dailies print a short list of the newer more actively traded issues. The table reveals the name, coupon rate, and maturity date of each issue, a representative price, change from the previous day, and the yield to maturity. An investor interested in obtaining specific quotes can refer to a publication such as *The Blue List.* Dealers will give quotes, but they may vary, depending on such factors as the dealer's profit margin.

36

FINANCIAL FUTURES

A futures contract is an agreement between seller and buyer to respectively deliver and take delivery of a commodity at a specified future date. Financial futures are futures contracts written on securities, money, or various stock indexes. Investors can use positions in the futures market to protect the gains they have made in the cash market. Speculators can also use futures to profit from anticipated changes in financial markets. Futures are not recommended for individual investors. The majority of individual investors lose money. Some are ruined.

Financial futures are traded on a regulated exchange complete with established rules for the performance of contracts. The exchange clearing-house acts as a third party and guarantor to all transactions, thus eliminating the need for sellers and buyers to become known to one another. While a future is a commitment to buy or sell at some point in the future, delivery of the underlying instrument rarely occurs. Trades in futures contracts are settled by entering into the offsetting position.

Reading Futures Quotes. Exhibit 14 provides an example of a futures listing. The following terms are used in the exhibit:

Open. Price at which the first bids and offers were made or first transactions were completed.

High. Top offer or top price at which a contract was traded during the trading period.

Low. Lowest bid or the lowest price at which a contract was traded.

Settlement. Price brokers use for valuing portfolios.

Net change. Amount of increase or decrease from the previous trading period's settlement price.

Life-of-contract highs and lows. Highest price or offer and the lowest price or bid reached in the lifetime of a futures contract for a specific delivery month.

Volume. Number of contracts traded (one side of each trade only) for each delivery month during the trading period.

Open interest. Accumulated total of all currently outstanding contracts (one side only) in futures. It refers to unliquidated purchases and sales.

Arithmetic of Financial Futures Trading. Perhaps more than any other form of speculation or investment, gains and losses in futures trading are highly leveraged. The leverage of futures trading results from the fact that only a small amount of money (called margin) is required to buy or sell a futures contract. The smaller the margin in comparison to the value of the futures contract, the greater the leverage. The term margin as used in connection with securities refers to the cash down payment a customer deposits with a broker when borrowing from the broker to buy securities. However, when applied to futures, margin is a deposit of good faith money that can be used by the brokerage firm to cover trading losses. It is analogous to money held in an escrow account.

EXHIBIT 14

Financial Futures Price Quotations

	Open	High	Low	Settle	Change	Lifetime High	Low	Open Interest
JAPANESE YEN (IMM) 12.5 million yen; $ per yen (.00)								
June	.7648	.7657	.7636	.7643	− .0007	.8485	.7500	47,806
Sept	.7749	.7759	.7740	.7744	− .0008	.8580	.7690	1,604
Dec	.7845	.7855	.7845	.7845	− .0009	.8635	.7735	391
Est vol 17,965; vol Fri 30,955; open int 49,884, +343.								
W. GERMAN MARK (IMM) — 125,000 marks; $ per mark								
June	.5416	.5427	.5408	.5410	+ .0007	.5975	.5317	51,358
Sept	.5461	.5473	.5454	.5458	+ .0008	.5977	.5366	878
Dec	.5505	.5520	.5505	.5506	+ .0007	.5895	.5430	207
Est vol 21,845; vol Fri 42,475; open int 52,443, +1,051.								
CANADIAN DOLLAR (IMM) — 100,000 dlrs.; $ per Can $								
June	.8404	.8411	.8402	.8409	....	.8433	.7670	19,168
Sept	.8367	.8370	.8365	.8371	− .0001	.8385	.7990	1,238
Dec	....	....	....	.8335	....	.8370	.7920	435
Est vol 2,346; vol Fri 5,152; open int 20,893, +1,051.								
BRITISH POUND (IMM) — 62,500 pds.; $ per pound								
June	1.7000	1.7092	1.6996	1.7060	+ .0080	1.8370	1.6200	22,195
Sept	1.6900	1.6984	1.6894	1.6944	+ .0080	1.8030	1.6580	351

Source: *The Wall Street Journal*

The exchange on which the contract is traded sets minimum margin requirements, typically about 5% of the current value of the futures contract. If the funds in an investor's margin account are reduced below what is known as the *maintenance level,* the broker will require that additional funds be deposited. Also, the investor may be asked for additional margin if the exchange or brokerage firm raises its margin requirements. Requests for additional margin are known as *margin calls.*

37

COMMODITY FUTURES

A commodity futures contract is a contract covering the purchase and sale of physical commodities for future delivery on a commodity exchange. The futures contract requires the future seller to deliver to a designated location a specified quantity of a commodity to be sold to the future buyer at a stipulated price on some defined later date. Originally, the purpose of futures was to transfer risk from one party to another and to smooth out price fluctuations. Subsequently, speculation has become an important factor in these markets. Commodity futures are used primarily by four groups of people.

Producers, including farmers, use the futures market to lock in the prices they receive for their products.

Commercial consumers use futures to insulate themselves from wide swings in the prices of the commodities they use.

Investors use futures as an opportunity to speculate on future price changes, up or down. These speculators theoretically assume the price risk that the hedger is seeking to minimize.

Finally, exchange floor traders are middlemen, buying from producers and selling to users.

The Futures Marketplace. The commodity futures market is very close to being a purely competitive market, with prices being determined by demand and supply. Usually a variety of forces exists at any one time to move prices up or down. These forces can involve a range of political, social, and economic factors in addition to factors peculiar to the particular commodity. Gold is an example of a commodity whose price is strongly influenced by political factors. However, for most agricultural commodities, fluctuating supplies largely determine prices.

Futures markets function as a form of forward pricing rather than substituting for the actual purchase or sale of a commodity. In fact, only about 2% of all futures contracts result in delivery.

Reading Futures Prices. Exhibit 15 is an example of how futures prices are reported. The top bold-faced line gives the name of the commodity, here, corn. Also listed is the exchange (CBT) which stands for the Chicago Board of Trade. Finally, the line lists the size of a single contract (5,000 bushels) and the way in which prices are quoted (cents per bushel).

The first column gives the months in which the delivery of the contract may occur. The next three columns give the opening, highest, and lowest prices of the day. A blank indicates that a particular month hasn't traded that day. The fifth column gives the settlement price, the price brokers use for valuing portfolios and for deciding whether to call for more margin. The change column shows the difference between the latest settlement price and that for the previous day. The second and third columns from the right display the highest and lowest prices at which each contract has ever traded. The right-hand column reveals the open interest in the column. Open interest is a measure of the public interest in a contract. Generally, the higher the open interest, the more liquid is the contract—that is, the easier to trade. The bottom line gives the volume of contracts traded, the previous day's volume, the total open interest, and the change from the previous day.

EXHIBIT 15

Commodities Futures Prices

CORN (CBT) 5,000 bu.; cents per bu.

Dec	239	239½	238	238¼	+ ¼	295	218½	100,254
Mr90	242½	243	241½	241¾	+ ¼	286½	226	60,677
May	246½	247	245¼	245½	....	289½	230	15,622
July	249¾	250¼	248½	248¾	....	285	231	15,054
Sept	243½	244	242½	242½	− ¼	271	229	955
Dec	240½	240¾	239	239¼	− ½	263½	222	5,337
Mr91	....	....	....	246	− ½	255	241	112

Est. vol. 34,000; vol. Fri 54,058; open int 198,011, + 2,653.

Source: *The Wall Street Journal*

38

GOLD

In early 1993, gold prices increased 15% from $326 to $375 in only a two-month period. Gold-mining stocks did even better, with some increasing more than 50%. Although many analysts were predicting further rises, gold bugs—investors with a fanatical devotion to gold—have in the past frequently been disappointed.

From 1934 to 1971, the U.S. maintained a policy of buying and selling gold at a fixed price of $35 per ounce. This policy prevailed until the Nixon administration suspended the dollar's convertibility into gold in 1971. Thus the value of gold is now determined by market forces. In the 1970s the price of gold zoomed upward and peaked in 1980 at $570 an ounce before falling to $308 in 1984. Since then, its price has generally fluctuated between $350 and $425 per ounce.

For 5000 years, gold has been more of an alternative currency than a commodity. Its universal acceptability has been due to its relative scarcity as well as its glitter.

Although estimates can be made of changes in supply, predicting demand is much more difficult. Over 50% of the gold produced is used for decorative purposes, 20% for official coins, 20–25% for industrial uses, and the remainder for private investment holdings. Gold has become a barometer for confidence in political and currency stability. When inflation heats up, demand for gold increases. Purchases of gold also surge when political events take a serious turn. Finally, high interest rates on money market instruments and securities make them more attractive as investments than gold since its ownership yields no interest. All of these factors make forecasting gold prices very difficult.

How to Purchase Gold. If an investor wants to buy gold to ensure against economic instability or to diversify holdings, there are six major avenues that can be pursued: mutual funds, gold stocks, coins, bullion, futures contracts, and options.

South Africa is the source of close to half the world's production of gold. The unstable political situation in that country makes investment in South African mining companies a risky business at best, but there are many North American companies listed on stock exchanges and available in over-the-counter markets. There are also mutual funds that invest in the stocks of these gold-mining companies.

Gold coins are issued by several governments which guarantee their gold content. These coins come in various weights and sizes. Some have a pure gold content while others consist of gold mixed with copper. Gold coins are sold at a price that reflects their gold value plus a premium of from 5% to 8%. The most prominent gold coins are the U.S. Gold One Ounce, South African Krugerrand, Canadian Maple Leaf, Austrian 100 Corona, and the Gold Mexican 50 Peso.

Gold bullion comes in many sizes ranging from a tiny wafer to 400-ounce bars. Most investors don't actually take physical possession of the bullion. Instead they purchase a certificate of ownership that indicates the gold is on deposit in a bank. Certificates can be purchased from certain banks, large brokerage houses, and recognized dealers.

Gold futures contracts are speculations that provide a lot of leverage. Typically, the cash requirements are 4% to 10% per contract. If the price falls, the investor is susceptible to a margin call for more cash or collateral. Most speculators lose money.

Gold options don't face the possibility of margin calls. Maximum risk is defined by the premium paid for the option. Like futures, the leverage is high and the profit potential large. However, as with futures, most speculators in options lose money.

Is Gold a Smart Investment? In response to concern about the federal deficit and increasing inflation, both the prices of gold and bullion and gold stocks have risen in early 1993. If you assume the federal deficit, inflation, and currency instability will be continuing economic problems, gold is a wise investment since it does best in times of greatest economic instability. However, most experts recommend investing only 5% to 10% of personal savings in gold investments because of their volatility and high risk.

39

CORPORATE DIVIDENDS

Dividends are distributions to stockholders. Although most commonly in the form of cash or stock, dividends may consist of property. Typically, corporations can only declare dividends out of earnings, although some state laws and corporate agreements permit the declaration of dividends from sources other than earnings. Dividends based on sources other than earnings are sometimes described as liquidating dividends because they are a return of the stockholder's investment rather than of profits.

Cash dividends are usually paid on a quarterly basis shortly after the dividend resolution has been approved by the board of directors. Dividends cannot be paid immediately because the ongoing purchases and sales of the corporation's stock require that a current list of stockholders be prepared. For example, a resolution approved at the April 10 (declaration date) meeting of the board of directors might be declared payable on May 5 (payment date) to all stockholders of record as of April 25 (record date). In this instance, on April 26, the day after the record date, the stock would trade ex-dividend, usually falling in price to compensate for the fact that it no longer qualifies for the latest dividend. News of corporate dividends is reported daily in *The Wall Street Journal* and the financial pages of larger newspapers.

Although about 60% of the average corporation's earnings is typically paid out in the form of cash dividends, the percentage payout varies widely. Smaller, high-growth companies tend to have lower payout ratios than mature companies. Generally, new companies have a stronger need to reinvest the cash generated from operations to finance growth.

Dividend Yield. The dividend yield percentage is often reported in the stock tables of major newspapers. This number is obtained by dividing the annual cash dividend by the closing price of the stock. The annual cash dividend is based upon the rate of the last quarterly payout. If the dividend in the last quarter was $.25 per share, the annual dividend is assumed to be $1.00.

Stock Splits and Stock Dividends. A stock split is the issuance to stockholders of new shares of stock. A 2 for 1 split, for example, gives each stockholder 2 new shares for each of the old shares. A stock dividend is simply a small stock split. For example, if a corporation issues a 5% stock dividend, the owner of 100 shares will receive an additional 5 shares of stock. Stock dividends like cash dividends trade ex-dividend after the record date. Stock that is split trades both on the presplit basis and on a when issued (wi) basis between the declaration date and the record date. Thus, a $100 stock split that was 2 for 1 would carry a $50 wi price.

Essentially, all that happens with these operations is that the total number of shares outstanding increases while the total value of the owners' common stock remains unchanged.

40

CORPORATE ACCOUNTING AND REPORTING

Accounting is the language of business and financial statements and represents a primary medium that corporations use to communicate their progress and performance. Financial statements are issued in a summarized form on a quarterly basis, and complete financial statements with notes are issued annually. Most analysts regard financial statements as a vital source of information about a firm. This key presents a discussion of two of the three basic financial statements, Income Statement and the Statement of Cash Flows. The Balance Sheet is discussed in Key 42.

Income Statement. Why is the income statement so important? The primary reason is that it provides investors, creditors, and others with information to help predict the amount, timing, and uncertainty of future cash flows. Accurate prediction of future cash flows permits the assessment of the economic value of the firm, the probability of loan repayment, and the probability of dividend payout.

Financial Ratios. Although there are many financial ratios used by analysts, some of the most prominent ones are based on amounts reported in the income statement. The most widely publicized of all financial ratios, earnings per share, is discussed in the next key. Other prominent ratios using income statement values are as follows:

- *Gross profit margin.* This ratio is computed by dividing gross profit by net sales for the period. The equation for this relationship is:

$$\text{profit margin on sales} = \frac{\text{gross profit}}{\text{net sales}}$$

This ratio measures the ability of the company to control inventory costs and to absorb price increases through sales to customers.

- *Return on common stock.* This measure is the ultimate measure of operating success to owners. It is calculated by dividing net income by the equity of common stockholders. In equation form:

$$\text{Rate of return on common stock equity} = \frac{\text{net income} - \text{preferred dividends}}{\text{common stockholders' equity}}$$

(To obtain common stockholders' equity, it is necessary to subtract from total stockholders' equity the stockholders' equity that pertains to preferred stock.)

- *Price earnings ratio.* The P/E ratio is widely used by analysts in assessing the investment possibilities of different stocks. It is computed by dividing the market price of the stock by the earnings per share:

$$\text{P/E ratio} = \frac{\text{Market price of stock}}{\text{Earnings per share}}$$

High P/E stocks are usually characterized by greater growth potential than low P/E stocks.

- *Payout ratio.* The payout ratio is the ratio of cash dividends to net income.

$$\text{Payout ratio} = \frac{\text{Dividends per share}}{\text{Earnings per share}}$$

Many investors select securities with a fairly substantial payout ratio. However, other investors are more concerned with growth in sales and profits, leading to appreciation in the price of the stock. High growth companies tend to be characterized by low payout ratios because they reinvest most of their earnings.

Statement of Cash Flows. The adoption of this statement in 1988 was spurred by the dissatisfaction of many investors with reported earnings as a measure of a firm's performance. Reported earnings are affected by choices made in the accounting methods used and may not be indicative of the underlying cash flows.

The primary purpose of this statement is to report information about a company's cash receipts and cash payments. It is useful because it provides information about the following issues:

1. Sources of cash.
2. Uses of cash.
3. Change in cash balances.

41

CORPORATE EARNINGS

Earnings per share (EPS) is probably the most publicized and relied-upon financial statistic. The financial dailies report earnings for most listed and OTC corporations as they are announced. Corporations are required by the SEC to report EPS to their stockholders every three months. Reported earnings can have at least a short-term impact on the price of a stock, particularly when they differ from expectations.

EPS has been called a summary indicator because as a single item it communicates substantial information about a company's performance or financial position. However, misleading inferences can be drawn if the calculations that derive EPS on the income statement are ignored. Further, analysis of a company's total operations and financial condition requires more information than can be garnered by simply examining EPS.

The term "earnings" is synonymous with "net income" and "net profit" to accountants who compute EPS. Earnings per share is the net earnings remaining for common stockholders after dividends due to the preferred stockholders:

$$\frac{\text{Net Income} - \text{Preferred Dividends}}{\text{Average Common Shares Outstanding}} = \text{EPS}$$

Two EPS numbers must be computed if a company has extraordinary gains or losses included in net income. This requirement provides information useful to investors by eliminating the distorting effect of extraordinary items upon EPS. By definition, extraordinary items represent events that are both unusual in nature and infrequent in occurrence. Typically, then, in making assessments of earnings performance, attention should be focused upon EPS resulting from normal operations, rather than gains or losses not expected to recur.

Complex Capital Structure. The calculation of EPS becomes more complicated when companies have convertible securities, stock options, warrants, or other financial

EXHIBIT 16

Earnings Report

AGP & CO. (O)

6 mo June 30:	1993	1992
Revenues	$4,856,859	$5,469,163
Net income	395,347	234,741
Avg shares	1,918,696	a1,860,186

Shr earns (com & com equiv):

Net income .	.22	a.13

a-Adjusted to reflect a one-for-three reverse split effective October 1992.

ARX INC. (N)

Quar June 30:	1993	1992
Sales	$20,841,000	$18,858,000
Income	1,137,000	530,000
Extrd cred	....	a280,000
Net income	1,137,000	810,000
Avg shares	8,756,000	8,724,000

Shr earns (primary):

Income	.13	.06
Net income .	.13	.09

Shr earns (fully diluted):

Income	.11	.06
Net income .	.11	.09

Year:

Sales	67,338,000	63,118,000
Income	2,236,000	725,000
Extrd cred	....	a280,000
Net income	2,236,000	1,005,000
Avg shares	8,757,000	8,661,000

Shr earns (primary):

Income	.26	.09
Net income .	.26	.12

Shr earns (fully diluted):

Income	.24	.09
Net income .	.24	.12

a-Tax benefit from tax-loss carryforwards.

ABRAXAS PETROLEUM (O)

Quar Jun 30 :	1993	1992
Revenues	$2,011,862	a$402,649
Net income	105,201	(43,104)
Avg shares	1,552,440	979,481

Shr earns:

Net income .	.03	(.11)

6 months:

Revenues	3,055,218	a937,779
Income	16,002	(8,244)
Extrd cred	2,229,964	....
Net income	2,245,966	(8,244)
Avg shares	1,520,456	979,481

APPLIED MATERIALS INC. (O)

13 wk Aug 1:	1993	a1992
Sales	$281,370,000	$193,789,000
Net income	28,173,000	10,692,000
Avg shares	41,266,000	35,902,000

Shr earns (com & com equiv):

Net income .	.68	.30

40 weeks:

Sales	752,636,000	540,904,000
Net income	65,187,000	26,469,000
Avg shares	41,028,000	35,562,000

Shr earns (com & com equiv):

Net income .	1.59	.7⬦

a-For 13 and 39 weeks.

ARROW TRANSPORTATION (O)

Quar Jun 30:	1993	1992
Revenues	$5,867,000	$6,326,000
Net income	300,000	160,000

Shr earns (com & com equiv):

Net income .	.10	.06

6 months:

Revenues	11,564,000	11,919,000
Net income	394,000	221,000

Shr earns (com & com equiv):

Net income .	.14	.08

ARTRA GROUP INC. (N)

Quar Jun 30:	1993	1992
Sales	$37,625,000	$48,052,000
aIncome	(2,663,000)	(7,788,000)
Extrd cred	b22,041,000	
Net income	19,378,000	(7,788,000)

Shr earns:

Income	(.59)	(1.88)
Net income .	4.03	(1.88)

6 months:

Sales	78,563,000	103,141,000
aInco cnt op ..	(3,642,000)	(10,896,000)
Inco dis op	....	330,000
Income	(3,642,000)	(10,566,000)
Extrd cred	b22,041,000	
Net income	18,399,000	(10,566,000)

Shr earns:

Inco cnt op .	(.84)	(2.65)
Income	(.84)	(2.57)
Net income .	3.78	(2.57)

a-Includes charges of $950,000 in the quarter and six months from restructurings, compared with reorganization charges of $456,000 and $672,000, respectively. b-Gain from forgiveness of debt.

Source: *The Wall Street Journal*

instruments that can be exchanged for or converted to common shares at some future time. The presence of these securities means that there is a potential increase in the number of common shares outstanding. In the computation of EPS, an increase in the number of shares outstanding results in a reduction (or dilution) of EPS. (See Exhibit 16 for sample earnings reports from *The Wall Street Journal.*)

If companies possess a complex capital structure, a dual presentation of EPS is required. Accountants refer to these EPS figures as "primary earnings per share" and "fully diluted earnings per share." Where large amounts of convertible securities are present, the assumption of full dilution can significantly reduce EPS.

Conclusion. Investors must be careful not to rely too heavily on EPS as reported in the financial press. Details in the income statements, such as trends in gross margin, may be more important than EPS. In addition, EPS may reveal little about the financial condition and cash flows of the firm. This information is generally presented in the annual and quarterly reports that a corporation issues. However, EPS can often be a valuable guide to evaluating a single firm's comparative performance over time. Since EPS is affected by the choices of accounting methods, and one firm's choices may be quite different from those of another firm, comparisons of EPS between firms should be made with caution.

42

BALANCE SHEET

The balance sheet is a document that reveals the financial condition of a company at a particular point in time. This statement summarizes what a firm owns (assets), what a firm owes to outsiders (liabilities), and the interests of the owners of the enterprise (owners' equity or stockholders' equity). In equation form, the balance sheet can be represented as follows:

$$\text{Assets} = \text{Liabilities} + \text{Stockholders' Equity}$$

By definition, the balance sheet must always balance, meaning the total balance for assets must always equal the total balance of the sum of liabilities and stockholders' equity. Thus, when a corporation increases its assets and/or decreases its liabilities, stockholders' equity grows.

Assets can be divided into three categories:

1. Current assets—cash plus other assets generally expected to be converted into cash within one year.
2. Property, plant, and equipment—assets with relatively long lives.
3. Intangible assets—valuable rights that have no physical substance, such as patents and copyrights.

Balanced against assets are liabilities, which are economic obligations of two types: current (generally payable within one year) and long-term.

Financial Ratios. Many financial ratios that are widely reported in the financial press are computed based upon the values on the balance sheet.

- *Book value per share.* Book value is defined as a company's total assets less its total liabilities. Many investors look for undervalued companies and possible takeover candidates by buying stocks that are selling below book value. They typically focus upon "tangible" book value, excluding such intangibles as patents and goodwill. This value becomes less relevant if the valuations on the balance sheet do not approximate the current market value of the assets.

- *Debt ratio.* This value is computed by dividing total liabilities by total assets. This ratio indicates the extent of the firm's financing with debt. The use of debt involves risk because it requires fixed interest payments and eventual repayment of principal. Particular attention should be paid to the debt ratio when considering troubled companies. Debt is a primary determinant of which companies will survive and which will go bankrupt in a crisis.
- *Current ratio.* This ratio is the most commonly used measure of short-run liquidity. It is measured by dividing current assets by current liabilities. It is important as an indication of the company's ability over the next 12 months to meet its obligations and still have sufficient resources to run its business effectively. There is no single "correct" current ratio; the figure varies from industry to industry.

43

MERGERS AND ACQUISITIONS

A merger occurs when one firm absorbs another firm and the latter loses its corporate identity. The terms "mergers" and "acquisitions" are now used interchangeably on Wall Street. There are many different ways to effect business combinations. Deals may involve stock acquisition, asset acquisition, or a combination of the two. In a stock acquisition, the acquiring firm (or individual) obtains controlling interest in the voting stock of the acquired firm and absorbs that firm. In an asset acquisition, the acquiring firm directly purchases the assets of the acquired firm. "Merger" is often combined with "acquisitions" and abbreviated as M & As. When "takeover" is used in the context of M & As, it implies that the acquired firm's management opposed the acquisition.

Current Merger and Acquisition Activity. The total value of acquisitions increased from $20 billion in 1976 to over $200 billion in 1988, the year giant deals were announced almost daily. The fall of 1988 produced a $5.2 billion acquisition of Pillsbury by Grand Metropolitan P.L.C. (a British company), a $13.1 billion takeover of Kraft by Philip Morris, and the record bidding contest for RJR Nabisco that culminated in a bid by a financial group, Kohlberg Kravis Roberts & Co. (KKR), of $25 billion, almost twice as large as the previous record for a takeover. Previously, M & A activity had been dominated by structured acquisitions intended to gain market share or expand product lines, paid for largely in cash or stock. The takeover mania of the 1980s, however, was often financed with enormous debt.

In 1990, 1991, and 1992, takeover activity slowed dramatically because financing was so much more difficult to obtain from both the banks and savings and loans. However, the M & A business in 1993 started picking up steam again. Second-quarter 1993 domestic merger and acquisition announcements were up 28% over the 1992 period to an early $50 billion. Reminiscent of the giant deals of the 1980s, Merck & Co., the world's largest drug company, agreed to buy Medco Containment Services, Inc., the nation's largest marketer of discount prescription medicines, for $6 billion in stock and cash.

In order to gain control of a company, a buyout specialist will generally make a tender offer to all the stockholders of a company to purchase a specified number of shares at a specified price within a specified time frame. The offer may come from the company itself or from another company or investor group. Tender offers are often part of hostile takeovers. The tender offer price is generally substantially above the current price to encourage shareholders to tender their shares. The stock price will spurt in response to the tender offer but will settle at a level slightly below the tender offer price. This gap arises because of the possibility that the takeover will fail.

Arbitrageurs often dominate the trading in a stock for which a tender offer has been made. These speculators try to buy a stock for less than they will ultimately be paid by the acquirer. Ivan Boesky was an arbitrageur before he was convicted of illegal trading in stocks. Boesky often bought shares in a company before a tender offer was publicly announced, using illegally obtained inside information.

Takeover Terminology. Takeover mania in the 1980s has spawned a colorful vocabulary, mostly reflecting the efforts of companies to fend off corporate raiders. Some terms that have become commonly used in the financial press are *poison pill,* a tactic designed to make a hostile takeover more expensive; *white knight,* a person or corporation who saves a corporation from a hostile takeover by taking it over on friendlier terms; *golden parachute,* lucrative severance pay or stock allowances for top executives concerned about their positions; *greenmail,* a concept similar to blackmail that refers to a corporation's buying back stock from a potential acquirer at a price that substantially exceeds the going market price; and *shark repellent,* wherein a potential takeover target enhances its defenses by the inclusion of corporate bylaws designed to put obstacles in the path of a takeover.

Leveraged Buyouts. A leveraged buyout (LBO) is a type of acquisition undertaken by a firm's managers with financing from a bank or investment group. Essentially, management buys the company's shares with borrowed money. Debts are paid from the company's cash flow. In addition, parts of the acquired company may be sold off to reduce debt. The term "leveraged" is appropriate because the majority of the new company's capitalization is debt. Later, the firm's stock may be sold to the public again or to another investment group, often producing tremendous profits for the managers and their bankers. If successful, the financial rewards can be awesome. The investors who put $80 million into Dr Pepper in 1986 received more than $600 million in cash in 1988.

44

INVESTMENT SCAMS

Every year the financial media reports on some investment scam that has duped unwary investors. Investors continually put their money in scams that clearly ought to arouse suspicion. In 1988 some publications carried advertisements offering to sell gold for $250 an ounce—$170 below the then market price. The catch was that the ore was still in the ground, and getting it into bullion form would cost more than it was worth. These schemes are believed to rake in an estimated $2 billion per year.

Ponzi Schemes. A 30-year-old immigrant, Charles Ponzi, etched his name in the annals of history in 1920 when he made an offer thousands of investors could not refuse—a 50% return in just six weeks. By the time the scheme began to unravel six months later, Ponzi had pocketed $10 million. His name has become synonymous with confidence games in which some early investors earn excellent returns, paid off with funds obtained from later participants in a scheme, who lose everything. Variations on the Ponzi scheme have duped investors over and over again. A late-1980s example that received widespread publicity was a game called "Airplane," which involved payoffs of up to $12,000 for anyone willing to risk $1,500. Here's how it worked: a "pilot" antes up $1,500 and persuades two "copilots" to do the same and recruit four "crew members," each of whom signs up two "passengers." With fifteen participants and a $22,500 kitty, the organizer deplanes with half the proceeds. The remainder belongs to the copilots, who now advance to pilots, with new passengers needed to keep the game going. Like all Ponzi schemes, this scheme crashes when the demand for new players exhausts the supply. This type of scheme is also called a "pyramid scheme" and is strictly illegal in most states.

Multilevel Marketing. Multilevel marketing (MLMs) companies strive to sign up thousands of salespeople who in turn sign up even more salespeople, hoping to share in their commissions. Some MLMs are illegal pyramid schemes because distributors generate their revenues primarily by collecting fees for signing up new distributors, who in turn collect fees by bringing in still more distributors. In these MLMs selling the product is actually a secondary purpose. A recent example of an MLM, United Sciences of America (USA), sold dietary products endorsed by celebrities. USA had a 16-member executive advisory board of doctors and scientists. Seven months after it was launched in January 1986, USA had signed up 140,000 distributors and was adding 10,000–15,000 new ones each month. Company executives projected sales would top $100 million in 1986 and $1 billion in 1989. This confidence game didn't last long. In October 1986, the NBC television network aired a critical report. USA's checks to its distributors started bouncing in December 1986. At that time, the Food and Drug Administration issued a regulatory letter challenging the claims made for four USA products. Within a few weeks, USA filed for bankruptcy protection under Chapter 11.

Other Scams. Any investment that guarantees an unusually high rate of return should be regarded with extreme caution. In 1992, securities investigators closed down Viscon Television Inc., a Wooster, Ohio firm that sold fraudulent investments in air time on cable and low-power television stations. The investors were told they could double their money in sixty days because the air time would be resold at higher prices to people marketing unique gadgets. Fraud seems to be rampant in such areas as art, coins, and limited partnerships. The penny-stock market has been a continuing source of headaches to state securities regulators. Investors are continually bilked by swindlers who prey on those who substitute greed for sound judgment. The emergence of computerized dialing and cheap long-distance phone rates has allowed smooth-talking brokers working out of "boiler rooms" to contact millions of people. They offer stock in small companies for a few cents per share, promising huge profits in a short time. Investors should be wary of the penny-stock market.

Of course, there are legitimate penny-stock offerings, but these are only for speculators who are able to absorb the inevitable losses in the hope of finding a big winner. Penny-stock quotes will not be found in newspapers but are published in "pink sheets," which are available at brokerage firms.

A useful preinvestment tool is now available for individual investors. Investors can obtain information about past disciplinary actions against brokers, or their firms, by calling 800-289-9999 between 8 a.m. and 4 p.m. every business day.

45

ASSET ALLOCATION

Most investors believe that the most important investing decision they make is the selection of individual stocks, bonds, mutual funds, and so forth. However, these decisions are not nearly as important as generally assumed. The asset allocation decision—how you split your dollars among stocks, bonds, and cash (including money market funds and short-term CDs)—is by far the most important determinant of investment performance. It turns out that what portion of your total assets is invested in stocks is generally far more important than the individual stocks you select.

Although the importance of asset allocation over individual security selection may surprise you, this is not news to the academics who researched this issue. One recent study by Brinson, Singer, and Beebower (published in the May–June 1991 issue of *Financial Analysts Journal*) assessed the performance of eighty-two large pension funds over a ten-year period. Their research shows that asset allocation determines more than 90% of the total return. The individual stocks and the other assets that the pension funds picked did little on average to improve performance over the ten-year period.

Many financial newsletters in recent years have increasingly emphasized asset allocation as an approach to investment. Although you might perceive it as a gimmick to sell financial products, they are on to something investors can ignore only at their own peril.

Most investors tend to pay little or no attention to how they allocate their assets. All too often, they own a hodgepodge of mutual funds or common stock bought at various times without consideration of how they complement each other. That is a big mistake. Proper attention to asset allocation can enable you to substantially enhance your return with little or no increase in risk.

The twenty-five-year compound annual total return (1968–1992), including price changes and reinvested dividends, for common stock (as measured by the Standard & Poor's 500 Index) is 10.56%. But the average return masks some years of glittering returns and other years that were real downers. Total returns soared more than 30% in five of the years but stocks were losing investments in six other years, including the 26.47% plunge in 1974. Some investors may not be comfortable with the level of volatility or risk. Those investors who plan to cash in their stocks to finance the college educations of their children or for their retirement in a few years may find the possibility of a 26.47% plunge unacceptable.

That's where asset allocation comes in. Consider what would have happened if an investor had put a third of his or her money in stocks, a third in Treasury bonds, and a third in a cash equivalent investment such as Treasury bills. In the twenty-five-year period, that investor would have lost money only four times, and the largest loss would have been less than 5%. Meanwhile, the compound annual return over the twenty-five years would have been 9%, compared with 10.56% for an all-stock portfolio. Thus, historically, sacrificing a 1.56% total return has been accompanied by dramatically reduced risk.

If you are interested in making the most money possible, and your time horizon is thirty to forty years, then investing entirely in stocks makes sense. Although you have a 30% chance of loss in any one-year period (based on results over the last sixty years), your risk drops to 15% over any five-year holding period and only 4% in any ten-year periods. In other words, extending the amount of time invested in the stock market greatly reduces risk.

But most investors have shorter time horizons, and investing totally in stocks is too risky. For them, investing in several classes of assets such as stocks, bonds, real estate (at least your own home), and cash equivalents is a better approach.

The best mix of investments will vary depending upon your age, income, health, employment stability, family size, and tolerance of risk. Each investor has to structure a strategy that fits his or her own personal circumstances, and this strategy will change as you get older and your financial position changes.

In making asset allocation decisions, you should get an overview of how the three major categories (stocks, bonds, cash) have performed historically. Stock and bond averages and indexes can provide this perspective.

Current index information is readily available in local and national newspapers and magazines. The best periodical for historical information remains the weekly publication, *Barron's* (1-800-228-6262).

The most complete information giving year-by-year total returns from 1926 for various stock and bond groups, as well as compound annual returns for different holding periods, is the yearly book, *Stock, Bonds, Bills, and Inflation,* published by Ibbotson Associates (1-312-616-1620). The 1993 yearbook costs $80. This publication is available at many libraries.

46

SOURCES OF INFORMATION

The purpose of this key is to describe the primary sources of information available to assist investors in making decisions. An investor does not need to read all the sources to make informed choices. However, it is necessary to be aware of trends in the economy and business activity. Most successful investors have a broad knowledge of the business and investment environment, so that they are capable of making judgments independent of the so-called experts. Such knowledge is important because the opinions of experts are frequently contradictory.

The most accessible source of information for nearly all investors is the financial pages of newspapers. Newspapers vary in their coverage of financial developments from excellent to poor. Both *The New York Times* and *USA Today* have excellent financial sections. Many investors choose to supplement their local newspapers with a specialized financial newspaper such as *The Wall Street Journal,* by far the most widely read daily financial newspaper. *Investor's Business Daily* is also useful, particularly to those investors who employ technical analysis (predicting future stock prices by using charts).

Many general business periodicals and financial magazines are also available. *Business Week, Fortune,* and *Forbes* are three major business magazines. *Business Week* is more oriented toward news reporting than the other two periodicals. In contrast, *Forbes* and *Fortune* (both published biweekly) focus on specific companies and business personalities. Investors should examine these periodicals and subscribe to at least one that appears most useful in enhancing their understanding of the securities markets. *Barron's,* the weekly sister publication of *The Wall Street Journal,* provides a wealth of useful financial data as well as columns and features on events significant to investors. *Money* carries many articles on investments and is a useful source of information on all aspects of financial planning.

Forbes, Business Week, and *Money* regularly devote issues to mutual funds. In the fall of each year, *Forbes* has an honor roll for mutual funds that have been the most successful performers. *Kiplinger's Personal Financial Magazine* gives excellent coverage to mutual fund investing. Every quarter, *Barron's* prints Lipper Analytical Services' mutual fund performance data plus numerous articles on mutual fund investing. Three excellent mutual fund reference sources are available at many public libraries: *Weisenberger Investment Company Service, Morningstar Mutual Funds,* and *The Handbook for No-Load Fund Investors.*

Standard & Poor's and Moody's are the two most important firms in the investment information business. They compete with a broad array of products covering the entire investment arena. Standard & Poor's publishes a series of *Standard Stock Reports,* which are usually available at brokerage firms. These one-page reports provide a useful summary and description of a firm's operations and financial history. For investors in bonds, it publishes the *Bond Guide,* which provides relevant information on thousands of corporate and convertible bonds.

Probably the most influential single stock advisory service is *The Value Line Investment Survey.* This publication is available at many public libraries. It provides a one-page summary of useful financial data on individual companies. Included is a ranking on a 1-5 scale of timeliness and safety. Timeliness means the probable price performance relative to the market over the next twelve months. Safety means the stock's future price stability and the company's current financial strength. A rank of 1 is the highest. This systematic approach lets the investor know exactly how Value Line regards the prospects of each firm.

Morningstar Mutual Funds (1-800-876-5005) does for mutual funds what the *Value Line Investment Survey* (1-800-833-0046) does for common stocks. It gives comprehensive fund coverage and currently tracks more than 1,000 mutual funds—both load and no-load, equity and fixed income (including municipal bond funds). Each mutual fund has its own one-page summary, updated periodically. This summary includes information such as rankings against other funds, top holdings and how they have changed recently, the fund's performance vs. the S & P 500, or a bond index, and an evaluation of the fund's performance based on a 1-5 scale.

QUESTIONS AND ANSWERS

How does the Fed regulate money supply?

First, the Fed buys and sells U.S. Government securities in the open market. When it buys securities, the Fed injects money into the banking system, allowing banks to lend more money and thus increase the money supply. The converse is true for the selling of securities. Second, the Fed regulates reserve requirements for the banks. If the reserve requirement goes up, the percentage of deposits at a bank that can be lent out goes down, thereby reducing the money supply. This route is not as flexible as open market trading, and is therefore used less often.

What are the differences among the major stock exchanges?

The New York Stock Exchange (NYSE) is the oldest exchange and has the most stringent listing requirements. To be listed on the NYSE, a corporation must have pretax earnings of $2.5 million for the preceding year as opposed to the $750,000 required by the American Stock Exchange (Amex). The corporation's net worth must be $18 million for the NYSE but only $4 million for the Amex. In addition, the NYSE has stronger requirements for the number of publicly held common shares and for trading volume.

Shares for many small corporations are traded on the Amex and on the regional exchanges, so that prices are more volatile than on the NYSE. The NYSE has the highest daily trading volume, followed by the Midwest Stock Exchange and the Amex.

What do the terms EPS and PE mean?

EPS is *earnings per share* calculated by subtracting preferred stock dividends from net income and dividing the remainder by the average number of common shares outstanding for the year. Annual EPS is often considered a summary indicator because it presents substantial information on the firm's performance in a single item.

If there are any extraordinary gains or losses in the year, that portion of EPS is calculated separately to eliminate the distortion they may lend to the annual earnings. If a firm has issued convertible securities or other financial instruments that can be exchanged for or converted into common shares, EPS must be computed to show the possible dilution of EPS by such conversions.

Investors must be careful not to rely too heavily on EPS, because details such as gross margin on sales, working capital ratios, and cash flows are not reflected in EPS. Therefore, EPS is more valuable as a guide to evaluating a firm's performance over time than as a basis for comparison among different firms.

PE is *price-earnings ratio,* which is the market price of a stock divided by its annual EPS. Thus, PE is a good indicator of how investors regard a company's (or the overall market's) prospects. Growth stocks generally have higher PEs than the shares of public utilities, for example, and PEs in general are higher in bull markets than in bear markets.

What do corporate bond ratings signify?

Several rating agencies, most notably Moody's and Standard & Poor's, assign bonds to different risk classifications. These classifications indicate the credit quality of the bond and the issuing company, which is one of the important factors in determining the interest rate the bond must carry to attract investors. Bonds rated AAA by Standard & Poor's or Aaa by Moody's are the highest-grade obligations, meaning they possess the ultimate degree of protection as to payment of principal and interest.

What do the primary stock market averages and indexes measure?

The Dow Jones Industrial Average is the most widely followed average. The 30 corporations measured by the DJIA are large "blue-chip" companies. The stock averages are price-weighted, meaning that the component stock prices are added together and divided by a particular divisor. Dow Jones also publishes group indexes covering several different industries.

The Standard & Poor's 500 Index (also called the Composite Index) is the second most widely followed index. On a daily basis, it is more representative of the movement of the stock market as a whole because it uses a larger sample—500 stocks—and it is market weighted according to the total value of the shares.

The NYSE Common Stock Index is also market weighted, as it reflects the overall changes of all common stocks on the Exchange by measuring the aggregate market value of NYSE common stocks (i.e., multiplying the price per share by the number of listed shares). The NYSE also computes group indexes for industrials, utilities, transportation, and financial stocks. The Amex Market Value Index is computed similarly to the NYSE Index but measures all the issues on the Amex.

How is inflation measured?

Inflation is difficult to measure accurately, because price changes for all goods in the economy cannot realistically be measured. Therefore, inflation must be estimated using a market basket of goods. The Consumer Price Index (CPI) measures changes in the prices of goods and services purchased by urban consumers, based on approximately 400 common items. The CPI is considered the most reliable measure of changes in the cost of living. The Producer Price Index (PPI), which used to be called the Wholesale Price Index, similarly measures items purchased by producers and other businesses. Imperfect as these measures are, they are widely followed by financial analysts.

What is full employment?

Full employment does not mean zero unemployment, because there will always be a certain number of people moving from one job to another or entering the work force and the job search for the first time. In the 1960s, full employment was said to be achieved at 4% unemployment; economists now estimate that the figure is closer to 6%. The higher the figure is thought to be due to (1) the larger number of wage earners per household, (2) higher unemployment benefits, and (3) more part-time job seekers. In general, it is thought that when unemployment drops below the full-employment number, wage inflation results.

Can a high U.S. deficit cause the federal government to go bankrupt?

No. First, when government debt becomes due, expenditures and taxes are not generally adjusted to retire the debt. Rather, new debt is issued, and the proceeds pay off the existing debt. Second, the federal government can "print more money"—that is, increase the money supply—which can be used to retire the debt. If this power is abused, skyrocketing inflation can result, but the U.S. government cannot go bankrupt as long as it has this power. The only portion of the debt that many economists regard as troublesome is the amount held by foreign investors, because payment of that portion represents the transfer of funds out of the American economy. As of 1993, approximately 15% of U.S. debt was held by overseas accounts, up from 5% in the 1960s.

How is an individual's investment in a corporation affected in a leveraged buyout?

A leveraged buyout occurs when management coordinates with an independent investment group to form a holding company that buys out the original stockholders. If your investment is in common stock, you will likely be offered considerably more than the market value of your stock to sell it. However, this may not be the case if your investment is in corporate bonds. Typically, 90% or more of the funds for the buyout are borrowed, thus "leveraging" the company and making it vulnerable to earnings downturns. This can greatly increase the risk of default for all corporate creditors, including the bondholders, causing the value of the bonds you hold to decrease in market value.

What does the Index of Leading Economic Indicators tell me?

The index can provide valuable information about the future path of the economy. It generally grows at a rate of 3% per year, about the same rate as the economy. If the index declines for several consecutive months, it is an indicator that a recession is forthcoming. Conversely, if the index grows faster than 3%, rapid growth in the future may be expected. There are shortcomings in the index, and many argue that a broader index should be constructed. Most importantly, it should be noted that long-term trends in the index are far more indicative of movement in the economy than are any month-to-month fluctuations.

When are stocks assets on the balance sheet and when are they stockholders' equity?

When a corporation holds shares of another company's stock as an investment, the holding is classified as an asset. Whether it is classified as a current asset or a long-term investment depends upon the intent of management. For it to be a current asset, the intent must be to sell it within the next year.

When a corporation issues its own common or preferred stock, it is classified on the balance sheet as stockholders' equity. The number of shares sold as well as the number of shares authorized to be sold must be disclosed. The shares are shown at par value, and if the stock was sold above par value, which is usually the case, the additional amount is shown as "paid in capital in excess of par." Treasury stock represents stock that had been sold at one time but that has been repurchased by the company.

What is the current ratio?

The current ratio is the most commonly used measure of short-run liquidity. It is computed by dividing the total current assets by the total current liabilities. Current assets consist of cash, marketable securities, receivables, and inventories, as well as any other assets expected to be used up within one year. Thus, all current assets are not equal. A company with a huge cash balance may be attractive to corporate raiders, while a company with a high inventory balance may simply be carrying a load of unsalable goods. Similarly, current liabilities are those payable within one year, usually including accounts payable from the purchase of goods and services as well as any notes payable coming due in the next year.

Is the gross profit on sales the same as net income?

No. Gross profit on sales represents sales revenue minus cost of goods sold. Cost of goods sold only includes the cost of materials or inventory and related freight expenses. A company incurs many other expenses such as salaries, travel, utilities, office supplies, employee benefits, taxes, etc. It also may earn income unrelated to sales. Net income represents all revenues minus all expenses for the year.

Is it important to me when the dollar rises or falls against foreign currencies?

Yes, for varying reasons. When the dollar declines in value, imported goods tend to be more expensive, thus adding to inflation. (Theoretically, then, a Japanese automobile should cost twice as much when the dollar can be exchanged for 120 yen than when the rate is 240 yen. In practice, when the dollar did drop between 1984 and 1988, Japanese auto companies cut costs and slashed profit margins in order to keep the prices of their products competitive.) Another result of a drop in the dollar is that U.S. goods become cheaper in overseas markets. At the same time, however, Americans traveling abroad found that their dollars bought less—especially in Japan and northern Europe—and foreign investors bought out many U.S. companies and assets such as real estate with "cheap" dollars.

GLOSSARY

Acquisition combination of firms in which the acquiring firm obtains controlling interest in the voting stock of the acquired firm.

Assets economic resources expected to provide future benefits to a firm

Balance sheet provides information about the assets, liabilities, and owners' equity of a company as of a particular date.

Bond ratings system of evaluating the credit quality of bonds by assigning the bonds to different risk classifications.

Call option right of a buyer to purchase a specified quantity of a security interest at a fixed price at any time during the life of the option.

Closed-end mutual fund a fund that offers a fixed number of shares that are traded on exchanges like stocks and bonds.

Commodity futures agreement to purchase or sell a specific amount of a commodity at a particular price on a stipulated future date.

Common stock fractional shares of ownership interest in a corporation.

Consumer price index a measure of prices at the consumer level for a fixed basket of goods and services.

Convertible security a bond or share of preferred stock that can be exchanged into a specified amount of common stock at a specified price.

Corporate bond long-term IOU of a corporation, secured by specific assets or a promise to pay; generally issued in units of $1000.

Coupon rate (stated rate) specified rate of interest that a corporation will pay its bondholders expressed as an annual percentage of face value.

Deficit the amount by which outlays and expenditures exceed receipts and revenues.

Discount rate rate of interest charged by the Federal Reserve to member banks.

Dividend payment to stockholders distributed from a corporation's earnings.

Earnings per share amount of net income attributable to each share of common stock.

Face value (par value, maturity value) amount the corporation must repay on the maturity date.

Federal funds rate interest rate paid by banks when borrowing from other banks' reserves.

Federal Reserve System central bank of the United States, which formulates monetary policy and controls the money supply.

Financial ratios indicators of a company's financial performance and position.

Foreign exchange rate price at which one currency can be traded for another.

Golden parachute lucrative compensation guaranteed top executives in the event of a takeover.

Greenmail purchase by a corporation of its own stock from a potential acquirer at a price substantially greater than the market price. In exchange, the acquirer agrees to drop the takeover bid.

Gross domestic product measurement of economic activity by computing the total market value of all goods and services produced in a given period.

Holding company investment company that owns a substantial ownership interest in other companies.

Income statement financial statement that shows a firm's revenues and expenses over a period of time.

Investment banking the industry that specializes in assisting business firms and governments in marketing new security issues.

Leverage accelerative effect of debt on financial returns.

Leveraged buyout (LBO) process of buying a corporation's stock with borrowed money, then repaying the debt from the corporation's assets.

Liabilities economic obligations of the firm to outsiders.

Liquidity the ease with which an asset can be converted into cash, reflecting a firm's ability to meet its short-term obligations.

Load fund type of mutual fund where the buyer must pay a sales fee, or commission, on top of the price.

Margin in *securities,* the amount of cash down payment and money borrowed from a broker to purchase stocks; in *futures,* a deposit of money that can be used by the broker to cover losses that may occur in trading futures.

Maturity date at which the principal amount of a bond is to be paid to the bondholder.

Merger combination of two or more firms into one.

Monetarist person who believes that the Federal Reserve's monetary policy, and not the government's fiscal policy, can control future levels of economic activity.

Monetary policy actions by the Federal Reserve to control the money supply, bank lending, and interest rates.

Money market mutual funds funds that invest in short-term debt instruments.

Money supply sum total of money in an economy, including currency held by the public plus transaction accounts in depository institutions and travelers checks.

Municipal bond tax-exempt security issued by state and local governments and local government agencies and authorities.

Mutual funds pool of commingled funds contributed by investors and managed by professional managers for a fee.

NASDAQ National Association of Securities Dealers Automatic Quotations; a computerized communications network that provides automated quotations (bid and asked prices) on stock.

Net asset value calculated by dividing the total assets of a fund by the number of mutual shares outstanding.

No-load fund type of mutual fund for which no fee is charged when it is initially issued.

Nominal interest rate rate of interest expressed in current dollars (not deflated for price level changes).

Open-end mutual fund fund that issues more shares as investors purchase more shares at a price equal to net asset value.

Over-the-counter market trades securities through a centralized computer telephone network that links dealers across the U.S.

Poison pill tactic used by corporations to defend against unfriendly takeovers, generally by making a takeover more expensive.

Preferred stock class of stock that has certain preferential rights over common stock.

Price-earnings ratio ratio of a share's market price to a company's earnings per share.

Prime rate interest rate charged by banks to their most creditworthy customers.

Productivity measure of the efficiency in the use of economic resources.

Put option right of a buyer to sell a specified quantity of a security interest at a fixed price at any time during the life of the option.

Real interest rate nominal rate of interest less the anticipated rate of inflation.

Securities and Exchange Commission U.S. Government agency that administers the federal laws that protect the investor.

Statement of cash flows financial statement that shows a firm's cash receipts and cash payments over a period of time.

Stock dividend pro rata distribution of additional shares of stock to stockholders.

Stock market averages index of the market prices of a specified number of stocks.

Stock table summary of the trading activity of individual securities.

Strike price exercise price, the price at which the stock or commodity underlying an option may be bought or sold.

Tender offer offer by one firm to the stockholders of another firm to purchase a specified number of shares at a specified price within a specified time frame.

Trade deficit amount by which the value of merchandise imports exceeds the value of exports.

Treasury securities debt obligations issued by the U.S. Government and backed by the full faith and credit of that government.

Warrant option to buy a specified number of common shares at a predetermined price within a fixed time period.

INDEX